Bristol Travel Guide 2025

Everything You Need to Know for an Unforgettable Bristol Experience

SAMUEL F. JUSTIN

Copyright © 2024 by SAMUEL FRANK JUSTIN

All rights reserved.

ISBN : 9798307533109

DEDICATION

To all the explorers, dreamers, and adventurers who seek to uncover the hidden gems of the world—this book is for you. May it inspire you to wander the streets of Bristol with curiosity, embrace its history with awe, and savor every moment of your journey.

A special thanks to the people of Bristol, whose warmth, creativity, and rich culture have made this city an unforgettable destination. Your stories and spirit are the heart of this guide.

To my family and friends, for their unwavering support and encouragement, and for always being my travel companions in spirit.

And to the city of Bristol itself, for offering endless inspiration and the promise of discovery at every turn.

Happy travels.

CONTENTS

INTRODUCTION

HISTORICAL BACKGROUND
- Notable Historical Sites and Landmarks
- Stories of Maritime Bristol

GEOGRAPHY AND CLIMATE
- Location and Layout of the City
- Seasonal Highlights: Best Time to Visit

RESTAURANTS IN BRISTOL
- Top Local Restaurants: Flavors of Bristol
- Vegan, Vegetarian, and Gluten-Free Options in Bristol
- Budget-Friendly Eats: Meals Under £15 in Bristol
- Fine Dining Recommendations: Luxurious Experiences in Bristol

BEST CUISINE TO TRY IN BRISTOL
- Must-Try Dishes: Bristol Specialties
- Recipes to Recreate the Taste of Bristol
- Cost of Dining Out in Bristol: From Budget to High-End
- Drinks and Desserts Unique to Bristol

TRANSPORTATION
- Getting to Bristol: Air, Rail, and Road Options
- Navigating the City: Public Transportation Tips
- Taxi and Ride-Share Costs

PRACTICAL ADVICE
- Safety Tips for Travelers
- Language and Communication in Bristol
- Emergency Contacts and Services in Bristol

VISA UPDATES AND ENTRY REQUIREMENTS

How to Apply for a UK Visa: Step-by-Step Guide
When and Where to Apply for Visas
Additional Required Documents for UK Visa Applications
LOCAL CUSTOMS AND ETIQUETTE
Cultural Norms and Practices in Bristol
Dos and Don'ts for Visitors in Bristol
How to Blend in Like a Local in Bristol
INSIGHT TIPS
Budget-Saving Hacks for Travelers in Bristol
Hidden Gems Only Locals Know in Bristol
ADVENTUROUS ACTIVITIES
Exploring the Avon Gorge and Clifton Suspension Bridge
Kayaking and Paddleboarding in Bristol Harbour
Hot Air Balloon Rides: A Sky-High View of the City
ACCOMMODATIONS IN BRISTOL
Affordable Hostels and Budget Hotels in Bristol
Mid-Range and Luxury Hotels in Bristol
Quirky Accommodation in Bristol: Boats, Cabins, and Boutique Stays
Bristol's Best Resorts: Luxury Escapes
TOP ATTRACTIONS IN BRISTOL
Iconic Landmarks: Clifton Suspension Bridge and Bristol Cathedral
Bristol's Vibrant Street Art Scene: The Banksy Connection
Museums and Art Galleries
CURRENCY EXCHANGE
Local Currency: The Pound Sterling (£)
Best Places to Exchange Currency in Bristol
PACKING ESSENTIALS
Weekend Packing List: Light and Efficient
Essentials for a 5-Day and 7-Day Bristol Trip
Seasonal Clothing Tips for Your Bristol Trip
About the Author

INTRODUCTION

It all started with a random travel article. "The most vibrant city in the UK," it said, accompanied by a picture of the Clifton Suspension Bridge glowing under a golden sunset. The image struck a chord, but it wasn't until I read about Bristol's maritime history, thriving art scene, and culinary diversity that I felt a pull I couldn't ignore. I knew I had to experience this city for myself.

Funding the trip wasn't easy—I'd been saving for months, cutting back on little luxuries and selling a few unused items online to add to my travel fund. I researched budget-friendly accommodations and low-cost transportation options to make the most of my visit without breaking the bank. Looking back, every effort was worth it because Bristol delivered an experience I'll never forget.

Why Visit Bristol in 2025?

Bristol in 2025 is a city that's hitting its stride. It's a place where history meets innovation, a city that honors its past while confidently embracing the future. With its commitment to sustainability and community-driven initiatives, Bristol has become a global example of what a modern city can achieve.

This year is especially exciting, with new festivals, art exhibitions, and attractions popping up to celebrate Bristol's cultural legacy. Whether you're a history enthusiast, a foodie, or an adventurer, the city offers countless reasons to visit. Imagine exploring cobblestone streets lined with independent shops, dining at riverside restaurants serving local delicacies, or discovering the latest Banksy mural in the unlikeliest of places.

But Bristol isn't just about what you see—it's about what you feel. It's the warmth of its people, the hum of creativity in its neighborhoods, and the connection you forge with its soul.

Discovering Bristol: My Experience

The moment I arrived in Bristol, I was greeted by a unique energy. The air felt alive with possibility. My first stop was the harborside, where I wandered along the water's edge, soaking in the vibrant mix of old and new. Victorian warehouses had been transformed into trendy cafés and galleries, while boats bobbed peacefully on the water.

One of the highlights was a visit to the SS Great Britain, a historic ship turned museum that seemed to transport me back in time. As I explored its decks, I could almost hear the echoes of sailors and passengers who once journeyed across the seas.

From there, I ventured into the heart of the city, where every street corner seemed to hold a story. I joined a walking tour that showcased Bristol's street art, including pieces by the enigmatic Banksy. The murals were more than art—they were social commentaries, giving me a deeper understanding of the city's character.

The food scene was another revelation. I tried everything from classic fish and chips at a local pub to a vegan feast at a hip café. Each meal was a celebration of Bristol's diverse culinary influences. And the cider! Bristol's craft cider scene is unparalleled, and no visit is complete without sampling a pint.

A City That Inspires

What struck me most about Bristol was its ability to inspire. Every interaction, from a casual chat with a street vendor to a conversation with a tour guide, made me feel like I was part of something bigger—a community that values creativity, resilience, and progress.

For 2025, Bristol has a lineup of events that promises to be extraordinary. The Bristol Balloon Fiesta will light up the skies with its colorful displays, while the harborside will host music festivals and open-air markets. It's a year that encapsulates everything the city stands for: celebration, connection, and creativity.

An Invitation to You

Bristol isn't just a destination; it's an experience that lingers with you long after you've left. It's the kind of place that fuels your curiosity, leaves you in awe of its beauty, and inspires you to see the world differently.

So, why visit Bristol in 2025? Because it's a city that welcomes you with open arms, surprises you at every turn, and sends you home with a heart full of memories. Whether you're planning a weekend escape or a longer adventure, Bristol is ready to show you why it's one of the UK's most captivating cities.

Pack your bags and let the journey begin—you won't regret it.

HISTORICAL BACKGROUND

Bristol's history is like a rich tapestry, woven with threads of trade, exploration, art, and culture that stretch back over a thousand years. From its origins as a small Saxon settlement to its rise as a significant maritime hub, Bristol's story is one of resilience, innovation, and transformation. Walking through the city feels like stepping into a living museum where every cobblestone and building has a tale to tell.

Notable Historical Sites and Landmarks

Clifton Suspension Bridge

Arguably Bristol's most iconic landmark, the Clifton Suspension Bridge is more than just an engineering marvel—it's a symbol of the city's ambition. Designed by Isambard Kingdom Brunel and completed in 1864, the bridge spans the dramatic Avon Gorge, offering breathtaking views of the surrounding landscape. Whether you're standing on the bridge or admiring it from afar, it's impossible not to be struck by its beauty and historical significance.

Bristol Cathedral

Dating back to the 12th century, Bristol Cathedral is a stunning example of Gothic architecture. Originally founded as an Augustinian abbey, the cathedral's intricate stained glass windows, vaulted ceilings, and serene atmosphere make it a must-visit for history enthusiasts and lovers of art.

St. Mary Redcliffe Church

Described by Queen Elizabeth I as "the fairest, goodliest, and most famous parish church in England," St. Mary Redcliffe is a masterpiece of medieval architecture. Its towering spire, ornate carvings, and rich history reflect the wealth and importance of Bristol during the Middle Ages.

The Red Lodge Museum

Tucked away in the heart of the city, the Red Lodge Museum is a hidden gem that offers a glimpse into Bristol's past. Originally built in 1580, the lodge has been carefully restored to showcase period furniture, art, and architecture. Each room tells a different chapter of the city's history, from the Elizabethan era to the Georgian period.

Bristol Old Vic

As the oldest continuously operating theater in the English-speaking world, the Bristol Old Vic is a testament to the city's cultural heritage. Founded in 1766, the theater has hosted countless performances and remains a hub for creativity and storytelling.

Stories of Maritime Bristol

Bristol's maritime history is at the heart of its identity, shaping the city's development and global influence. Its strategic location on the River Avon made it a key trading port as early as the 11th century, connecting the city to Ireland, Europe, and beyond.

The Harbor and Its Transformation

Bristol's harborside was once a bustling center of trade, with ships carrying goods like wool, wine, and tobacco. The docks played a crucial role in the city's prosperity during the medieval period and later during the Industrial Revolution. Today, the harborside has been transformed into a vibrant cultural and leisure destination, but its history is still palpable in the cobblestones and restored warehouses.

The SS Great Britain

No exploration of Bristol's maritime past is complete without a visit to the SS Great Britain. Designed by Isambard Kingdom Brunel, this revolutionary steamship was the largest in the world when it launched in 1843. It crossed the Atlantic in just 14 days, marking a new era in ocean travel. Restored to its former glory, the SS Great Britain now serves as a fascinating museum that brings the city's maritime heritage to life.

The Transatlantic Slave Trade

Bristol's history is not without its darker chapters. During the 17th and 18th centuries, the city was a major hub for the transatlantic slave trade, with ships transporting enslaved Africans to the Americas. Today, Bristol acknowledges this painful past through museums and public discussions, ensuring that the lessons of history are not forgotten.

The Matthew

The Matthew is a replica of the ship that John Cabot sailed from Bristol to Newfoundland in 1497, marking one of the earliest European voyages to North America. Visitors can step aboard the ship at the harborside and imagine the daring spirit of exploration that defined Cabot's journey.

Making the Most of Your Time Exploring Bristol's History

To truly immerse yourself in Bristol's history, start your journey at the M Shed, a museum dedicated to the city's story. Here, you'll find exhibits that cover everything from medieval trade to contemporary culture. Next, take a stroll along the harborside, where plaques and restored buildings tell the tale of Bristol's maritime heyday.

For a deeper dive, join a guided walking tour focused on the city's historical landmarks. Knowledgeable guides can reveal hidden details and anecdotes that you might miss on your own. Don't forget to set aside time to explore the SS Great Britain, St. Mary Redcliffe, and the Clifton Suspension Bridge—all essential stops that showcase Bristol's rich and varied past.

Bristol's history isn't just something you learn about—it's something you experience with every step. From its role in shaping global trade to its enduring contributions to art and culture, the city offers a journey through time that will leave you with a profound appreciation for its legacy.

GEOGRAPHY AND CLIMATE

Location and Layout of the City

Bristol is a vibrant city in the southwest of England, strategically positioned where the River Avon meets the Severn Estuary. Its location has historically made it a key maritime hub, connecting the city to the Atlantic Ocean and facilitating trade with the Americas and Europe. This prime geographical position has significantly shaped its development, transforming it into one of the UK's most dynamic cities.

Nestled between rolling hills and open countryside, Bristol boasts a striking mix of urban landscapes and natural beauty. The city is surrounded by the Mendip Hills to the south and the Cotswolds to the east—both designated Areas of Outstanding Natural Beauty—offering stunning vistas and outdoor recreational opportunities. To the west lies the Severn Estuary, providing access to the Bristol Channel and the Welsh coastline.

The heart of the city is built along the River Avon, which cuts through Bristol in a dramatic gorge before flowing into the estuary. The Clifton Suspension Bridge, one of the city's most iconic landmarks, spans this gorge, connecting the affluent suburb of Clifton to Leigh Woods. The riverbanks, once bustling with trade, have been transformed into a lively harborside area, filled with restaurants, cultural attractions, and historic landmarks.

Bristol's layout is a testament to its rich history and modern growth. The historic Old City, with its medieval street patterns, contrasts sharply with the contemporary architecture of Cabot Circus, a bustling shopping and entertainment district. The city is divided into distinct neighborhoods, each with its own character and charm. From the colorful houses of Totterdown perched on the hills to the bohemian vibe of Stokes Croft and the Georgian elegance of Clifton, Bristol's diversity is reflected in its urban design.

The city's compact layout makes it relatively easy to explore on foot or by bike, though its hilly terrain can be challenging at times. Its extensive public transport network, including buses, ferries, and a growing cycling infrastructure, ensures connectivity across neighborhoods and beyond. The combination of historical landmarks, green spaces, and a vibrant urban core makes Bristol's layout both functional and picturesque, inviting exploration at every turn.

Seasonal Highlights: Best Time to Visit

Bristol's charm is ever-present throughout the year, but the city's seasonal highlights can make your visit particularly memorable depending on your preferences. Each season brings its own unique experiences, shaped by Bristol's temperate maritime climate, which ensures relatively mild winters and pleasant summers.

Spring (March to May)

Spring in Bristol is a time of renewal and vibrancy. The city's parks and gardens come to life with blooming flowers, and the countryside surrounding Bristol bursts into shades of green. Temperatures range from 8°C to 15°C (46°F to 59°F), making it an ideal time for walking tours, river cruises, and exploring outdoor landmarks like the Clifton Suspension Bridge and Ashton Court Estate.

Spring also brings festivals like the Bristol Walk Fest and the Foodies Festival, offering a taste of local culture and culinary delights. It's the perfect season for travelers who appreciate mild weather, fewer crowds, and the freshness of the city awakening from winter.

Summer (June to August)

Summer is peak tourist season in Bristol, and for good reason. With long daylight hours, temperatures averaging 17°C to 22°C (63°F to 72°F), and a packed calendar of events, the city is alive with energy. The iconic Bristol Harbour Festival, a celebration of the city's maritime heritage, takes place during this time and features live music, boat displays, and family-friendly activities.

The harborside buzzes with outdoor dining and street performances, while green spaces like Brandon Hill and Castle Park are perfect for picnics. For those interested in adventure, summer is ideal for cycling through the surrounding countryside or taking a hot air balloon ride during the Bristol International Balloon Fiesta, one of the city's most spectacular events.

Autumn (September to November)

Autumn in Bristol offers a quieter, more reflective charm as the summer crowds wane and the city takes on a golden hue. Temperatures cool to a comfortable range of 10°C to 15°C (50°F to 59°F), making it perfect for exploring Bristol's cultural landmarks and museums, such as the SS Great Britain and M Shed.

The changing colors of Leigh Woods and the Avon Gorge create breathtaking backdrops for hikes and photography. Autumn is also harvest season, and Bristol's vibrant food scene shines during events like the Bristol Food Connections Festival, where you can savor locally-sourced dishes and artisan treats.

Winter (December to February)

Bristol's winters are mild compared to many other destinations, with temperatures rarely dropping below 2°C (36°F) and averaging around 6°C to 8°C (43°F to 46°F). The festive season transforms the city into a magical wonderland, with Christmas markets at Broadmead and St. Nicholas Market offering handmade crafts, seasonal treats, and mulled wine.

Winter is the best time to experience Bristol's indoor attractions, from the awe-inspiring Bristol Cathedral to the immersive We The Curious science center. Cozy pubs with roaring fireplaces provide a warm respite after a day of sightseeing. For a unique experience, visit during January or February to catch the Bristol Slapstick Festival, a celebration of classic and modern comedy.

When to Visit

The best time to visit Bristol largely depends on your interests. For lively festivals and warm weather, summer is ideal, while spring and autumn offer a balance of comfortable temperatures and fewer crowds. If you prefer a more relaxed pace and festive cheer, winter brings a quieter yet enchanting side of the city.

Ultimately, Bristol's year-round appeal ensures there's never a wrong time to explore its history, culture, and vibrant community.

RESTAURANTS IN BRISTOL

Top Local Restaurants: Flavors of Bristol

Bristol is a city renowned for its eclectic culinary scene, blending traditional British fare with global influences. From cozy bistros to innovative fine dining, the city offers a wealth of options to tantalize your taste buds. Below is a curated list of some of the best local restaurants in Bristol, complete with location, opening hours, and a detailed overview of each.

1. The Olive Shed

Location: Princes Wharf, Wapping Road, BS1 4RN
Opening Hours:

- Monday–Thursday: 12 PM – 10 PM
- Friday–Saturday: 12 PM – 11 PM
- Sunday: 12 PM – 9 PM

Overview:
 Nestled along the harborside, The Olive Shed is a haven for Mediterranean-inspired cuisine. Known for its tapas, freshly prepared with local and seasonal ingredients, the restaurant offers a vibrant menu featuring dishes like grilled octopus, baked feta, and lamb kofta. With views of the harbor from its terrace seating, it's the

perfect spot for a leisurely lunch or a romantic evening. Vegetarian and vegan options are also plentiful, making it inclusive for all diners.

2. Pasture

Location: 2 Portwall Lane, BS1 6NB
Opening Hours:

- Monday–Saturday: 12 PM – 10 PM
- Sunday: Closed

Overview:
Pasture is a modern steakhouse with a farm-to-table ethos, highlighting the finest locally-sourced meats and produce. Known for its show-stopping dry-aged steaks, the menu also features an array of sides like truffle mac and cheese and coal-roasted vegetables. The restaurant's open kitchen adds an interactive element, allowing diners to watch chefs expertly prepare their meals. Pasture's sophisticated yet relaxed ambiance makes it a favorite for special occasions.

3. Adelina Yard

Location: Queen Quay, Welsh Back, BS1 4SL
Opening Hours:

- Wednesday–Saturday: 12 PM – 2:30 PM, 6 PM – 9:30 PM
- Sunday–Tuesday: Closed

Overview:
For a fine-dining experience, Adelina Yard delivers impeccable dishes crafted with innovation and artistry. This riverside restaurant specializes in modern European cuisine with a Bristolian twist, featuring a tasting menu that evolves with the seasons. Signature dishes like Cornish turbot or wild garlic gnocchi showcase the kitchen's creativity and dedication to quality. The intimate setting and attentive service ensure an unforgettable dining experience.

4. The Canteen

Location: 80 Stokes Croft, BS1 3QY
Opening Hours:

- Monday–Sunday: 10 AM – 11 PM

Overview:
A cornerstone of Bristol's artsy Stokes Croft neighborhood, The Canteen combines great food with live music and a community vibe. The menu changes daily but emphasizes sustainable, locally-sourced ingredients. Expect hearty dishes like vegan burgers, mezze platters, and homemade soups. The Canteen also has a strong focus on affordability, making it popular among students and families. Its eclectic lineup of live performances adds a unique cultural flavor to your dining experience.

5. Box-E

Location: Unit 10, Cargo 1, Wapping Wharf, BS1 6WP
Opening Hours:

- Wednesday–Saturday: 12 PM – 2 PM, 6 PM – 9:30 PM
- Sunday–Tuesday: Closed

Overview:
Box-E is a tiny yet mighty gem housed within a shipping container at Wapping Wharf. Its intimate setting, with just a handful of tables, allows the chefs to focus on delivering exquisite plates. The menu is rooted in modern British cuisine, with standout dishes like venison carpaccio and cider-braised pork belly. Reservations are essential due to its limited seating, and the personalized service ensures every guest feels special.

6. Casamia

Location: The General, Lower Guinea Street, BS1 6SY
Opening Hours:

- Wednesday–Saturday: 12 PM – 2 PM, 6 PM – 9 PM
- Sunday–Tuesday: Closed

Overview:
Casamia is the epitome of culinary sophistication, earning its reputation as one of Bristol's finest dining establishments. Offering a multi-course tasting menu, the restaurant explores bold flavors and intricate techniques. Each dish, from amuse-bouche to dessert, is a work of art. Situated in a historic hospital building, the minimalist interior design contrasts beautifully with the rich complexity of the food.

7. Thali Easton

Location: 64-66 St Mark's Road, BS5 6JH
Opening Hours:

- Monday–Sunday: 12 PM – 10 PM

Overview:
For those craving a taste of India, Thali Easton delivers vibrant flavors in a relaxed setting. Known for its signature Thali trays, which feature a selection of curries, rice, and sides, the restaurant focuses on authentic recipes with a modern twist. The Easton branch is a local favorite, offering an inviting atmosphere with colorful decor and warm service.

8. Bristol Loaf

Location: 199a Gloucester Road, BS7 8BG
Opening Hours:

- Monday–Friday: 7:30 AM – 6 PM
- Saturday–Sunday: 8 AM – 6 PM

Overview:
Bristol Loaf is a haven for artisanal bread, pastries, and brunch dishes. Located on the bustling Gloucester Road, it's an ideal spot for a casual meal or coffee break. Their brunch menu, featuring

dishes like avocado toast and shakshuka, pairs perfectly with locally-roasted coffee. Freshly baked goods, from croissants to sourdough, make it a must-visit for bakery enthusiasts.

9. The Gallimaufry

Location: 26-28 Gloucester Road, BS7 8AL
Opening Hours:

- Monday–Sunday: 12 PM – 12 AM

Overview:
Known affectionately as "The Galli," this eclectic restaurant and bar is a hub for good food, craft drinks, and live music. The menu focuses on seasonal, locally-sourced ingredients, offering inventive small plates like spiced cauliflower and duck liver parfait. With its quirky decor and lively atmosphere, The Gallimaufry is a true reflection of Bristol's creative spirit.

10. Poco Tapas Bar

Location: 45 Jamaica Street, BS2 8JP
Opening Hours:

- Wednesday–Saturday: 12 PM – 11 PM
- Sunday: 12 PM – 6 PM

Overview:
Poco Tapas Bar is a sustainable eatery that champions zero-waste dining. Offering a tantalizing selection of tapas inspired by global flavors, the menu changes daily based on available produce. Dishes like smoked mackerel pate and Moroccan lamb kofta showcase the chefs' flair for combining bold spices and fresh ingredients. Located in the heart of Stokes Croft, Poco is a testament to Bristol's innovative culinary ethos.

Bristol's diverse restaurant scene is a true reflection of the city's multicultural heritage and vibrant energy. Whether you're seeking an indulgent tasting menu or a cozy spot for comfort food, these top local restaurants promise a memorable culinary adventure.

Vegan, Vegetarian, and Gluten-Free Options in Bristol

Bristol is a haven for plant-based and gluten-free dining, offering a wide range of restaurants that cater to dietary preferences and restrictions. With its vibrant food scene, the city is packed with innovative eateries that serve delicious vegan, vegetarian, and gluten-free meals. Below is some of the best options in Bristol, complete with their location, opening hours, and a detailed overview.

1. Koocha Mezze Bar

Location: 203B Cheltenham Road, BS6 5QX
Opening Hours:

- Monday–Thursday: 5 PM – 10 PM
- Friday–Saturday: 12 PM – 10 PM
- Sunday: 12 PM – 9 PM

Overview:
Koocha Mezze Bar is a vibrant Persian-inspired vegan eatery that specializes in small plates bursting with bold flavors. Their menu includes a delightful array of mezze like spiced aubergine, falafel, and za'atar fries, all entirely plant-based and with plenty of gluten-free options. Located on the bustling Cheltenham Road, this colorful spot is perfect for sharing dishes with friends in a lively, welcoming atmosphere.

2. Oowee Vegan

Location: 65 Baldwin Street, BS1 1QZ
Opening Hours:

- Monday–Sunday: 12 PM – 10 PM

Overview:
Oowee Vegan has revolutionized the vegan fast-food scene with its indulgent burgers, loaded fries, and shakes. Their "Sneaky Clucker" burger, featuring crispy vegan fried chicken, is a crowd favorite. The menu also accommodates gluten-free diners with carefully marked options. With a central location on Baldwin Street, Oowee Vegan is a must-visit for those craving comfort food without compromise.

3. Cafe Kino

Location: 108 Stokes Croft, BS1 3RU
Opening Hours:

- Monday–Sunday: 9 AM – 6 PM

Overview:
Cafe Kino is a cooperative-run vegan café that emphasizes sustainability and community. Known for its hearty breakfasts, burgers, and fresh salads, the menu is entirely plant-based and includes gluten-free options. Their homemade gluten-free cakes and locally sourced coffee are a treat not to be missed. Located in the artistic Stokes Croft area, it's a great spot to relax while enjoying ethically sourced food.

4. Root

Location: Unit 9, Cargo 1, Wapping Wharf, BS1 6WP
Opening Hours:

- Tuesday–Saturday: 12 PM – 2:30 PM, 6 PM – 9:30 PM
- Sunday: 12 PM – 3 PM
- Monday: Closed

Overview:
Root offers an innovative approach to dining, with a menu focused on vegetables as the star ingredient. While not entirely vegan or vegetarian, most dishes are plant-based, and the restaurant provides excellent gluten-free options. Dishes like roast cauliflower with tahini and smoked aubergine with pickled chili highlight their

commitment to creative cooking. Situated in Wapping Wharf, Root's minimalist decor and riverside views add to its charm.

5. The Spotless Leopard

Location: Mobile Food Truck (various locations)
Opening Hours:

- Check social media for daily locations and hours

Overview:
The Spotless Leopard is a vegan food truck offering a rotating menu of hearty dishes like jackfruit burgers, vegan mac and cheese, and gluten-free brownies. Known for its dedication to sustainability and wholesome meals, this mobile eatery pops up at various locations around Bristol, including festivals and markets. Check their social media for updates on where to find them each day.

6. Earthcake

Location: 71 North Street, BS3 1ES
Opening Hours:

- Tuesday–Saturday: 10 AM – 5 PM
- Sunday: 11 AM – 4 PM
- Monday: Closed

Overview:
Earthcake is a vegan bakery and café that specializes in beautifully crafted cakes and pastries, many of which are gluten-free. Their menu features savory options like vegan quiches and soups, making it a perfect spot for brunch or a quick snack. Located on North Street, this cozy café is known for its friendly service and warm atmosphere.

7. VX Bristol

Location: 123 East Street, Bedminster, BS3 4ER
Opening Hours:

- Monday–Sunday: 11 AM – 9 PM

Overview:
VX Bristol is a plant-based junk food paradise, offering everything from vegan kebabs and nachos to decadent milkshakes. Their menu caters to gluten-free diners with marked options, ensuring everyone can enjoy their indulgent offerings. The quirky interior and upbeat vibe make it a favorite among locals and visitors alike.

8. Eat Your Greens

Location: 156 Wells Road, BS4 2AG
Opening Hours:

- Wednesday–Saturday: 10 AM – 11 PM
- Sunday: 10 AM – 5 PM
- Monday–Tuesday: Closed

Overview:
Eat Your Greens is a family-run eatery that combines a vegan café with a bar, offering a dynamic menu of plant-based dishes. Their seasonal offerings include everything from hearty stews to creative gluten-free desserts. The venue's relaxed, homey atmosphere makes it an excellent choice for a leisurely meal.

9. Poco Tapas Bar

Location: 45 Jamaica Street, BS2 8JP
Opening Hours:

- Wednesday–Saturday: 12 PM – 11 PM
- Sunday: 12 PM – 6 PM

Overview:
Poco Tapas Bar is celebrated for its sustainable and locally sourced approach to dining. While not exclusively vegan or vegetarian, their menu features plenty of plant-based and gluten-free tapas options, such as roasted beetroot hummus and spiced lentil fritters. The cozy atmosphere and commitment to zero-waste dining make it a

standout choice.

10. The Bristolian

Location: 2 Picton Street, BS6 5QA
Opening Hours:

- Monday–Sunday: 9 AM – 5 PM

Overview:
The Bristolian is a beloved café known for its generous portions and focus on inclusivity. Their menu offers a variety of vegan, vegetarian, and gluten-free breakfast and lunch options, such as vegan pancakes and gluten-free sandwiches. Located in the heart of Montpelier, this charming spot combines delicious food with a laid-back ambiance.

Bristol's diverse and inclusive food scene ensures that no dietary preference goes unmet. These top vegan, vegetarian, and gluten-free options provide something for everyone, allowing you to enjoy the city's culinary delights without compromise.

Budget-Friendly Eats: Meals Under £15 in Bristol

Bristol's vibrant food scene isn't just about high-end dining; it also offers a variety of budget-friendly options where you can enjoy delicious meals for under £15. From hearty breakfasts to flavorful street food, these eateries prove that good food doesn't have to break the bank. Here's a curated list of top budget-friendly spots.

1. The Canteen

Location: 80 Stokes Croft, BS1 3QY
Opening Hours:

- Monday–Sunday: 9 AM – 11 PM

Overview:
The Canteen is a cornerstone of Bristol's vibrant Stokes Croft neighborhood, offering affordable, locally sourced meals with a strong focus on sustainability. Their daily-changing menu often features hearty stews, curries, and salads, all priced under £10. The lively atmosphere, live music, and commitment to community make this spot a favorite among locals and visitors alike.

2. Matina

Location: St Nicholas Market, Glass Arcade, BS1 1LJ
Opening Hours:

- Monday–Saturday: 10 AM – 4 PM
- Sunday: Closed

Overview:
Matina is a must-visit for fans of Middle Eastern cuisine. Nestled in the bustling St Nicholas Market, this small eatery specializes in freshly made Kurdish flatbreads filled with grilled meats, vegetables, and flavorful sauces. Prices hover around £7, making it an excellent option for a quick and satisfying meal. Arrive early to avoid long queues during lunch hours.

3. Eat a Pitta

Location: Multiple locations, including Broadmead and St Nicholas Market
Opening Hours:

- Monday–Saturday: 10 AM – 5 PM
- Sunday: 11 AM – 4 PM

Overview:
Eat a Pitta is famous for its generously stuffed falafel pittas and salad boxes. Packed with fresh vegetables, homemade hummus, and crispy falafel, a meal here costs around £6–£8. With multiple

locations across the city, it's a convenient and affordable choice for a healthy, flavorful lunch.

4. Cafe Amore

Location: 14 Nelson Street, BS1 2LE
Opening Hours:

- Monday–Saturday: 8 AM – 6 PM
- Sunday: Closed

Overview:
Cafe Amore serves hearty breakfasts, sandwiches, and Italian-inspired dishes at wallet-friendly prices. Their full English breakfast, priced under £10, is a local favorite. The cozy interior, complete with eclectic decor, makes it a welcoming spot to relax and enjoy a meal.

5. Oowee Diner

Location: 46 Park Street, BS1 5JG
Opening Hours:

- Monday–Sunday: 12 PM – 10 PM

Overview:
Oowee Diner brings indulgent comfort food to the budget-friendly category. Their burgers and loaded fries, often priced around £12, are generously portioned and packed with flavor. Located on the iconic Park Street, it's a great stop after exploring the nearby attractions.

6. The Bristolian

Location: 2 Picton Street, BS6 5QA
Opening Hours:

- Monday–Sunday: 9 AM – 5 PM

Overview:
Known for its hearty portions and friendly atmosphere, The Bristolian offers meals that are both affordable and delicious. Their vegetarian and vegan breakfasts, priced under £10, are particularly popular. Nestled in Montpelier, this café is ideal for a casual brunch or lunch.

7. Pie Minister

Location: 24 Stokes Croft, BS1 3PR
Opening Hours:

- Monday–Saturday: 11 AM – 9 PM
- Sunday: 11 AM – 6 PM

Overview:
Pie Minister is a Bristol institution known for its gourmet pies served with mash, mushy peas, and gravy. Most meals cost under £10, making it a fantastic option for hearty, comforting food. Their Stokes Croft location is perfect for a quick meal in a casual setting.

8. Taka Taka

Location: 2a Queens Road, BS8 1QP
Opening Hours:

- Monday–Sunday: 11 AM – 10 PM

Overview:
Taka Taka serves up affordable Greek street food with generous portions. Their gyros wraps, priced at around £6, are packed with grilled meat or halloumi, fresh vegetables, and creamy tzatziki. Conveniently located near the University of Bristol, it's a popular choice among students and budget-conscious travelers.

9. Woky Ko: Kaiju

Location: Cargo 2, Wapping Wharf, BS1 6WD
Opening Hours:

- Monday–Saturday: 12 PM – 10 PM
- Sunday: 12 PM – 9 PM

Overview:
Woky Ko: Kaiju offers Asian-inspired street food with plenty of options under £15. Their bao buns and noodle bowls, filled with flavorful ingredients, are perfect for a quick yet satisfying meal. The waterfront location in Wapping Wharf adds to the dining experience.

10. The Coconut Tree

Location: 2 Byron Place, BS8 1JT
Opening Hours:

- Monday–Sunday: 12 PM – 10 PM

Overview:
The Coconut Tree brings a taste of Sri Lanka to Bristol with its selection of small plates, most priced between £3 and £8. Signature dishes like hoppers and kotthu are flavorful and affordable, making it a great spot for sharing multiple dishes with friends. The lively atmosphere and unique flavors make it a standout choice for budget-friendly dining.

11. Pieminister's Grab & Go

Location: Various kiosks and stalls around Bristol
Opening Hours:

- Hours vary by location

Overview:
For those on the move, Pieminister's Grab & Go stalls offer quick and affordable options. Their classic pies, priced around £4–£5, are perfect for a light meal or snack while exploring the city. Locations include key spots like Temple Meads station and Broadmead.

Bristol's culinary scene proves that you don't need to spend a fortune to enjoy fantastic food. These budget-friendly spots deliver exceptional flavors and experiences, all for under £15, making them perfect for travelers exploring the city on a budget.

Fine Dining Recommendations: Luxurious Experiences in Bristol

Bristol is not only known for its lively food scene but also for its collection of luxurious dining experiences that cater to those who appreciate refined tastes, sophisticated atmospheres, and world-class service. Here's a curated list of fine dining establishments in the city, each offering a unique culinary experience that's sure to impress.

1. The Glassboat

Location: Welsh Back, BS1 4SB
Opening Hours:

- Monday–Saturday: 12 PM – 10 PM
- Sunday: Closed

Overview:
Set aboard a charming converted Dutch barge, The Glassboat offers a stunning waterside view alongside exquisite contemporary British cuisine. With an emphasis on locally sourced ingredients, their menu features expertly crafted dishes such as pan-seared sea bass, roasted rack of lamb, and indulgent desserts. This romantic spot, which boasts an elegant yet relaxed atmosphere, is perfect for those seeking a refined dining experience with views of the river and city skyline.

2. Casamia

Location: 27 Southville, BS3 1DJ
Opening Hours:

- Wednesday–Saturday: 6 PM – 9:30 PM
- Sunday–Tuesday: Closed

Overview:
A Michelin-starred gem, Casamia is one of Bristol's most prestigious dining experiences. Headed by chef-patron Peter Sanchez-Iglesias, Casamia offers a tasting menu that showcases creative dishes with bold flavors, drawing inspiration from British and Mediterranean cuisines. The intimate and stylish setting adds to the luxury, making it ideal for a special occasion. With dishes that change seasonally, each visit promises a unique, innovative experience that will delight even the most discerning foodies.

3. The Pony & Trap

Location: Chew Magna, BS40 8TQ (just outside Bristol)
Opening Hours:

- Monday–Saturday: 12 PM – 2:30 PM, 6 PM – 9 PM
- Sunday: 12 PM – 4 PM

Overview:
Located just a short drive from central Bristol, The Pony & Trap is a Michelin-starred restaurant that combines the charm of a countryside pub with the sophistication of fine dining. Known for its farm-to-table approach, the restaurant offers an ever-changing menu with locally sourced meats, seasonal vegetables, and an outstanding wine list. This rustic yet elegant establishment is perfect for those looking to escape the city and indulge in a tranquil yet luxurious dining experience.

4. Restaurant Story

Location: 33-35 Prince Street, BS1 4PS
Opening Hours:

- Monday–Saturday: 12 PM – 2:30 PM, 6 PM – 10 PM
- Sunday: Closed

Overview:
Restaurant Story is an award-winning restaurant offering an exciting narrative-driven approach to fine dining. Their tasting menus change frequently, emphasizing modern British cuisine with creative twists, often featuring seasonal ingredients. The minimalistic and stylish interior allows the food to take center stage, offering a theatrical experience that engages all the senses. Ideal for a sophisticated dinner date or special celebration, Restaurant Story offers an unparalleled dining adventure.

5. The Royal York

Location: 100 Regent Street, BS8 1ES
Opening Hours:

- Monday–Friday: 7 AM – 10 AM, 12 PM – 3 PM, 6 PM – 9 PM
- Saturday–Sunday: 8 AM – 10 AM, 12 PM – 3 PM, 6 PM – 9 PM

Overview:
For a truly opulent experience, The Royal York offers both traditional elegance and contemporary flair. Situated within a beautifully restored Georgian building, the fine dining restaurant serves high-end British cuisine with a focus on seafood, dry-aged steaks, and seasonal produce. With impeccable service, an extensive wine list, and an art-deco interior, dining at The Royal York is nothing short of spectacular. Whether it's a celebratory dinner or an indulgent night out, this establishment promises a memorable experience.

6. The Ethicurean

Location: Barley Wood Walled Garden, Long Lane, BS40 5SA (on the outskirts of Bristol)
Opening Hours:

- Monday–Sunday: 12 PM – 10 PM

Overview:

The Ethicurean is a hidden gem located just outside Bristol, set within a beautiful walled garden. It focuses on sustainability and serving organic, locally grown produce. The restaurant offers a selection of seasonal tasting menus that highlight the best of British ingredients, often from the garden itself. With its rustic charm, The Ethicurean is perfect for those looking to experience a luxurious farm-to-table dining experience surrounded by nature. Its emphasis on ethical dining and sustainability adds to the sense of occasion.

7. Gordon Ramsay's Restaurant at the Avon Gorge Hotel

Location: Sion Hill, BS8 4LD
Opening Hours:

- Monday–Saturday: 12 PM – 3 PM, 5:30 PM – 9:30 PM
- Sunday: 12 PM – 3 PM

Overview:
Set in the stunning Avon Gorge Hotel, this Gordon Ramsay restaurant offers exceptional fine dining with a focus on classic French techniques and modern twists. With its elegant décor, sweeping views of the Clifton Suspension Bridge, and a menu featuring refined dishes such as truffle risotto and butter-poached lobster, dining here is a sophisticated treat. Ideal for those celebrating an occasion or looking to impress, this restaurant offers the kind of experience that makes Bristol a standout destination for luxurious dining.

8. The Olivette

Location: 41 Westbury Park, BS6 7JG
Opening Hours:

- Monday–Saturday: 12 PM – 2:30 PM, 5 PM – 9:30 PM
- Sunday: Closed

Overview:
The Olivette is a modern, intimate fine dining restaurant located in the picturesque Westbury Park area of Bristol. Known for its fusion

of Mediterranean and British cuisines, this eatery serves inventive dishes prepared with fresh, seasonal ingredients. Expect highlights like roasted venison with fig and port jus, and freshly made pasta paired with rich sauces. The charming atmosphere, combined with elegant service, ensures a luxurious yet welcoming experience.

9. The Star & Dove

Location: 47-49 South Parade, BS8 1QF
Opening Hours:

- Monday–Saturday: 12 PM – 11 PM
- Sunday: 12 PM – 9 PM

Overview:
For those seeking a sophisticated, laid-back fine dining experience, The Star & Dove is a hidden gem offering a refined pub menu with a twist. Their seasonal menu is thoughtfully designed to cater to contemporary tastes with a mix of fresh seafood, gourmet burgers, and classic roasts. With an extensive selection of cocktails and fine wines, The Star & Dove promises a casual but luxe experience perfect for those looking for something both elegant and unpretentious.

10. Aponte

Location: 100 Gloucester Road, BS7 8AE
Opening Hours:

- Monday–Saturday: 12 PM – 10 PM
- Sunday: Closed

Overview:
Aponte brings a taste of Southern Italy to Bristol, offering fine dining with an emphasis on regional Italian flavors. From homemade pastas to exceptional seafood dishes, the menu is a celebration of Italy's best ingredients. The cozy yet upscale interior, paired with excellent service, creates an atmosphere that is both luxurious and welcoming. Whether you're a fan of traditional Italian fare or enjoy

discovering innovative takes on classic recipes, Aponte provides an unforgettable fine dining experience.

Bristol's fine dining scene offers an impressive mix of innovative chefs, locally sourced ingredients, and sophisticated settings. Whether you're celebrating a special occasion or simply indulging in a luxurious night out, these restaurants promise an extraordinary culinary experience that's sure to delight.

BEST CUISINE TO TRY IN BRISTOL

Must-Try Dishes: Bristol Specialties

Bristol's food scene is as diverse and vibrant as the city itself, boasting a rich array of dishes that are a true reflection of its maritime history, multicultural influences, and commitment to locally-sourced ingredients. Here's a curated list of Bristol's must-try specialties, each offering a unique taste of the city, from savory classics to sweet indulgences.

1. Bristol-Cut Cider-Cured Ham

Where to Get It:

- **The Cider Press** (Stoke Bishop, BS9 1DJ)
- **The Lido Café** (Clifton, BS8 4SD)

Cost:

- Approx. £7–£10 per dish

Overview:
 A nod to Bristol's proud cider-making heritage, the Bristol-cut cider-cured ham is a local delicacy that combines the sweetness of

apples with the saltiness of dry-cured ham. The ham is marinated in local cider, imparting a unique flavor that is both tangy and savory. Served with freshly baked bread and seasonal greens, this dish is a perfect representation of the region's penchant for using local ingredients to create flavorful comfort food. The balance of sweet and savory flavors makes it an unforgettable experience for your taste buds.

2. Bristol Cream Tea

Where to Get It:

- **The Clifton Tea Rooms** (Clifton Village, BS8 4LB)
- **Harbourside Café** (Bristol Harbourside)

Cost:

- Approx. £6–£8 per serving

Overview:
A quintessential British treat, the Bristol Cream Tea features warm scones served with clotted cream and strawberry jam, paired with a steaming pot of traditional English tea. What sets the Bristol variation apart is the generous helping of homemade jam, often using locally grown fruit, and the creamy, luxurious scones. The addition of a drizzle of local honey or even a splash of Bristol's famous cider can add a touch of local flair. This dish offers a sweet, comforting taste of British culinary tradition with a local twist.

3. Bristish Scallops with Cider Reduction

Where to Get It:

- **The River Grille** (Bristol Harbourside)
- **The Ox** (Clifton, BS8 1AF)

Cost:

- Approx. £15–£20 per main course

Overview:
Bristol's coastal location means fresh, high-quality seafood is readily available, and one standout dish is the British scallops with cider reduction. These perfectly seared scallops are accompanied by a rich cider-based sauce that enhances their natural sweetness with the tangy notes of local cider. Paired with a creamy mash or delicate seasonal vegetables, this dish encapsulates the marriage of Bristol's maritime heritage with its love of locally made cider. The sweetness of the scallops combined with the deep, fruity cider sauce makes for an elegant, memorable dish.

4. Cheddar Cheese and Onion Pie

Where to Get It:

- **Pieminister** (St. Nicholas Market, BS1 1JH)
- **The Bristol Pie Co.** (Gloucester Road, BS7 8AE)

Cost:

- Approx. £4–£6 per pie

Overview:
Cheddar cheese, the pride of the West Country, is the star of this comforting dish. A rich and indulgent cheddar cheese and onion pie, often served with a side of mashed potatoes and gravy, is a beloved Bristol specialty. The sharpness of the cheese combined with the sweet, caramelized onions creates a perfect harmony of flavors. This hearty dish is ideal for a cozy lunch or dinner, offering both savory satisfaction and a warm, comforting feeling.

5. Bristolian Breakfast

Where to Get It:

- **The Boston Tea Party** (Bristol City Centre)
- **The Café at the Arnolfini** (Harbourside, BS1 5DB)

Cost:

- Approx. £10–£12 per serving

Overview:
A full Bristolian breakfast is a must-try for those who appreciate a hearty, fulfilling meal to start the day. Featuring a mix of locally sourced ingredients, this breakfast includes items like fried eggs, bacon, sausage, black pudding, grilled tomatoes, baked beans, and toast, all served with a side of potato hash. While it's similar to the traditional English breakfast, the local twist comes from the inclusion of regional specialties such as locally made sausages or the addition of Cotswold rarebit (a cheese toast). Sweet and savory in balance, this breakfast is both filling and flavorful.

6. The Bristol Bun

Where to Get It:

- **Bristol's Bakery** (King Street, BS1 4EQ)
- **The Famous Bristol Bakehouse** (Old Market, BS2 0JX)

Cost:

- Approx. £2–£3 per bun

Overview:
Sweet, soft, and buttery, the Bristol Bun is a beloved treat with a rich history. The bun, often studded with dried fruit and spiced with a touch of cinnamon or nutmeg, is glazed with sugar syrup to give it a shiny, sweet finish. The traditional recipe has evolved over time, but it's still a favorite for those visiting Bristol, especially when paired with a cup of coffee or tea. Its slightly spiced flavor and sweetness make it a perfect mid-afternoon snack, especially when you're exploring the city's historic streets.

7. Potted Shrimps on Toast

Where to Get It:

- **The Rummer Hotel** (St. Nicholas Street, BS1 1UB)

- **The Old Duke** (King Street, BS1 4EB)

Cost:

- Approx. £6–£8 per dish

Overview:
A classic dish with roots in the local fishing community, potted shrimps are a flavorful, unique specialty of the Bristol area. The shrimps are gently poached and then set in a spiced butter, served atop buttered toast. The resulting dish is rich, indulgent, and brimming with the fresh flavors of the sea. Paired with a refreshing pint of cider or a glass of wine, this dish makes for a truly authentic Bristolian experience, offering a taste of the city's deep maritime heritage in every bite.

8. Bristolian Cider and Pork Belly

Where to Get It:

- **The Beerd Bar** (Clifton, BS8 1QJ)
- **The Cider Tap** (King Street, BS1 4ER)

Cost:

- Approx. £14–£18 per main course

Overview:
A fusion of two of Bristol's finest offerings—cider and pork belly—this dish features tender, slow-roasted pork belly drizzled with a sweet cider glaze. The cider enhances the natural flavors of the meat, adding a tangy richness that complements the crispy skin. Served with seasonal vegetables and a side of mashed potatoes or apple sauce, this dish is a comforting and savory treat. It's the perfect way to enjoy two of the region's most famous culinary exports in one satisfying meal.

Each of these dishes offers a delicious glimpse into Bristol's culinary identity, from comforting pastries to world-class seafood. Whether you're savoring a sweet Bristol Bun or indulging in the hearty flavors of Cheddar cheese and onion pie, every bite in Bristol tells a story of the city's rich heritage and dedication to locally sourced ingredients. Don't miss out on these iconic tastes as you explore the vibrant food scene in one of England's most dynamic cities.

Recipes to Recreate the Taste of Bristol

Bristol's culinary scene is a blend of maritime history, local farming, and creative innovation. From hearty breakfasts to indulgent desserts, here are some recipes that bring the flavors of Bristol into your kitchen. Each recipe uses ingredients that reflect the region's taste, history, and local pride. So, grab your apron, and let's recreate the taste of Bristol!

1. Bristol-Cut Cider-Cured Ham

Ingredients:

- 500g of local dry-cured ham (or a good quality ham of your choice)
- 1 cup of dry cider (preferably from the West Country)
- 1 tbsp brown sugar
- 1 tbsp Dijon mustard
- 1 tsp smoked paprika
- Freshly ground black pepper
- A pinch of sea salt

Method:

1. **Marinate the Ham:** In a bowl, mix the cider, sugar, mustard, smoked paprika, pepper, and salt. Place the ham in a shallow dish, and pour the cider marinade over it. Cover and refrigerate for at least 4 hours or overnight to allow the

flavors to infuse.
2. **Cooking:** Preheat the oven to 180°C (350°F). Transfer the marinated ham to a roasting pan, reserving some of the cider marinade. Roast the ham for about 25-30 minutes, basting it with the marinade every 10 minutes.
3. **Serving:** Once the ham is golden and tender, slice it thinly. Serve with freshly baked bread, a light salad, or roasted root vegetables to enjoy the full Bristol experience.

Tip: This dish pairs beautifully with a glass of dry cider from the West Country for an authentic taste of Bristol.

2. Bristol Cream Tea

Ingredients for Scones:

- 225g self-raising flour
- 1 tsp baking powder
- 100g cold unsalted butter, cubed
- 25g caster sugar
- 1 large egg
- 150ml full-fat milk
- A pinch of salt

Ingredients for Clotted Cream & Jam:

- 250g clotted cream
- 200g strawberry jam (or raspberry jam for a twist)

Method:

1. **Making the Scones:** Preheat the oven to 220°C (200°C fan) or 425°F. In a large bowl, sift together the flour, baking powder, and salt. Add the cubed butter and rub it in with your fingertips until the mixture resembles breadcrumbs. Stir in the sugar.
2. **Add Wet Ingredients:** Beat the egg with the milk and gradually add to the dry mixture. Stir until a dough forms. Turn the dough onto a floured surface and gently knead it for

a minute or two.
3. **Shaping the Scones:** Roll the dough to about 2.5 cm (1 inch) thick and use a round cutter to shape the scones. Place them on a lined baking tray and brush the tops with a little milk for a golden finish.
4. **Baking:** Bake for 12–15 minutes until the scones have risen and are golden brown.
5. **Serve:** Let the scones cool slightly, then serve with a dollop of clotted cream and a spoonful of jam.

Tip: Enjoy with a pot of Earl Grey or traditional English tea for the full Bristol Cream Tea experience.

3. Cheddar Cheese and Onion Pie

Ingredients for Pastry:

- 225g plain flour
- 125g cold unsalted butter, cubed
- A pinch of salt
- 2-3 tbsp cold water

Ingredients for Filling:

- 200g mature cheddar cheese (preferably from the West Country)
- 2 large onions, finely chopped
- 1 tbsp butter
- 2 tbsp plain flour
- 300ml whole milk
- Salt and pepper to taste

Method:

1. **Making the Pastry:** In a food processor, pulse the flour, butter, and salt until the mixture resembles breadcrumbs. Slowly add the cold water, one tablespoon at a time, until the dough comes together. Wrap in plastic wrap and chill in the fridge for at least 30 minutes.

2. **Preparing the Filling:** In a pan, melt the butter over medium heat. Add the onions and cook for about 10 minutes until soft and golden. Stir in the flour and cook for a further 1–2 minutes.
3. **Add Milk and Cheese:** Slowly pour in the milk, stirring constantly to avoid lumps. Cook until the sauce thickens. Once thickened, stir in the grated cheddar and season with salt and pepper.
4. **Assembling the Pie:** Preheat the oven to 180°C (350°F). Roll out the pastry on a floured surface and line a pie dish. Fill with the cheddar and onion mixture, then cover with more pastry. Trim the edges, crimp the sides, and make a small hole in the center for ventilation.
5. **Baking:** Bake for 30–35 minutes, until the pie is golden brown and the filling is bubbling.

Tip: Serve with a simple side salad or mashed potatoes for a comforting meal that embodies Bristol's heart and soul.

4. Potted Shrimps on Toast

Ingredients:

- 200g cooked and peeled shrimp
- 50g unsalted butter
- 1 tbsp chopped fresh parsley
- 1 tsp lemon juice
- 1 tsp smoked paprika
- A pinch of salt and pepper
- Freshly toasted bread

Method:

1. **Preparing the Shrimp:** In a small saucepan, melt the butter over low heat. Once melted, add the smoked paprika and lemon juice, then stir in the shrimp and parsley. Cook gently for 2-3 minutes until the shrimp are well-coated and heated through.

2. **Serving:** Spoon the potted shrimp and buttery sauce over slices of freshly toasted bread. Sprinkle with a little extra parsley and serve immediately.

Tip: Potted shrimps can be made ahead of time and stored in the fridge, allowing the flavors to meld together for an even richer taste.

5. Bristolian Cider and Pork Belly

Ingredients:

- 1kg pork belly, scored
- 1 cup dry cider (local variety recommended)
- 1 tbsp honey
- 1 tbsp Dijon mustard
- 2 cloves garlic, minced
- Fresh thyme sprigs
- Salt and pepper to taste

Method:

1. **Preparing the Pork Belly:** Preheat the oven to 180°C (350°F). In a roasting pan, combine the cider, honey, mustard, garlic, and thyme. Place the scored pork belly in the pan, skin side up, and rub with salt and pepper.
2. **Roasting:** Roast the pork belly for about 1.5–2 hours, basting every 30 minutes with the cider mixture. After 1 hour, increase the heat to 220°C (430°F) for the final 30 minutes to crisp up the skin.
3. **Serving:** Once the pork belly is golden and the skin is crispy, carve into slices and serve with the cider sauce drizzled on top.

Tip: Pair this dish with roasted potatoes or braised vegetables for a full, satisfying meal.

Recreating these iconic Bristol dishes at home allows you to bring a little piece of the city's culinary magic into your own kitchen. Whether you're preparing a warm and hearty pie, indulging in sweet scones, or savoring fresh local seafood, these recipes bring Bristol's unique flavors to life. Enjoy the journey of cooking these dishes, and let the tastes of Bristol transport you straight to the heart of the city.

Cost of Dining Out in Bristol: From Budget to High-End

Bristol's food scene is rich and diverse, offering options for every budget. Whether you're looking for an affordable, casual meal or a luxurious dining experience, the city has something to suit your tastes and your wallet. Below is a curated list of dining options, ranging from budget-friendly eateries to high-end restaurants, each with a breakdown of their cost, atmosphere, and culinary offerings.

1. The Bristolian Café (Budget-Friendly)

Location: 3 Upper Perry Hill, Bristol BS8 1SR
Average Cost: £5 - £10 per meal
Overview:
The Bristolian Café is a charming local spot perfect for a hearty, affordable breakfast or lunch. This café specializes in freshly prepared comfort food using locally sourced ingredients. Expect delicious options like scrambled eggs with smoked salmon, grilled cheese sandwiches, and homemade cakes. It's a casual and cozy environment, ideal for a relaxed meal without breaking the bank.

Cuisine: The Bristolian is renowned for its traditional British comfort food with a modern twist.
Sweetness: While not heavily focused on sweets, their homemade cakes, especially the Victoria sponge, are a must-try for anyone craving a little sweetness.

2. Saffron (Mid-Range Dining)

Location: 3-5 Colston Street, Bristol BS1 5AR

Average Cost: £15 - £25 per person
Overview:
Saffron offers a contemporary take on Indian cuisine, blending traditional spices with modern techniques. The atmosphere is vibrant and welcoming, making it a great place for a casual but special dinner. The menu includes flavorful curries, rich biryanis, and freshly baked naan bread. Their signature Saffron Chicken Tikka and a variety of vegan options ensure there's something for everyone.

Cuisine: Indian-inspired dishes with bold, aromatic flavors.
Sweetness: The Mango Lassi here is a sweet, refreshing drink that pairs beautifully with the spice-forward dishes.

3. The River Grille (Mid-Range to High-End)

Location: The Bristol Marriott Royal Hotel, College Green, Bristol BS1 5TA
Average Cost: £25 - £40 per person
Overview:
The River Grille offers a refined dining experience with stunning views of the Bristol Harbour. This restaurant specializes in locally sourced seafood, premium cuts of meat, and fresh seasonal ingredients. Whether you're indulging in their pan-seared seabass or the signature dry-aged steak, The River Grille promises an upscale dining experience in an elegant setting. It's perfect for a special occasion or an intimate dinner.

Cuisine: British fine dining with a focus on fresh, local produce.
Sweetness: For dessert, the dark chocolate mousse with sea salt caramel is the perfect indulgence, balancing richness and sweetness.

4. Casamia (High-End Fine Dining)

Location: 21-22 The General Market, Bristol BS1 3AE
Average Cost: £75 - £120 per person
Overview:

Casamia is one of the top fine-dining establishments in Bristol, offering an exquisite and artistic tasting menu. The restaurant's approach to cuisine is both avant-garde and rooted in the region's finest ingredients. Their multi-course meals are carefully curated by expert chefs, and each dish is a piece of culinary art. Casamia's ambiance is sophisticated and contemporary, making it an ideal destination for food connoisseurs or those looking to celebrate a major event in style.

Cuisine: Modern European cuisine with a heavy focus on local and seasonal ingredients.
Sweetness: Their signature dessert, the "Peach & Thyme," is a delicate balance of fresh fruit, herbs, and sweetness, making for a memorable finish to the meal.

5. Pizzarova (Affordable Pizza)

Location: 62-64 North Street, Bristol BS3 1HJ
Average Cost: £7 - £12 per pizza
Overview:
For a more casual dining experience, Pizzarova serves up some of the best wood-fired pizzas in Bristol. The menu is filled with creative combinations, including their popular margherita pizza with buffalo mozzarella and fresh basil. The atmosphere is laid-back, with a modern interior and an open kitchen where you can watch the pizzas being made.

Cuisine: Neapolitan-style wood-fired pizzas with fresh, high-quality ingredients.
Sweetness: The Nutella pizza for dessert is a decadent treat, offering a sweet and indulgent way to end your meal.

6. The Pump House (Gastropub - Mid-Range)

Location: Hotwells Road, Bristol BS8 4RU
Average Cost: £15 - £30 per person
Overview:
The Pump House combines the charm of a traditional British pub

with the elegance of a gastropub. Located by the water, it offers an inviting atmosphere with classic British dishes elevated to an art form. Known for its excellent Sunday roasts, the Pump House also serves delicious fish and chips, as well as inventive pub classics like slow-cooked lamb shoulder and beer-battered haddock.

Cuisine: British gastropub fare with an emphasis on fresh, local produce.
Sweetness: The sticky toffee pudding here is an absolute must-try, served warm with a rich toffee sauce and a scoop of vanilla ice cream.

7. The Lido (High-End Experience)

Location: Oakfield Place, Bristol BS8 2BJ
Average Cost: £30 - £60 per person
Overview:
The Lido, located in a restored Victorian outdoor swimming pool, offers a truly unique dining experience. The restaurant features a Mediterranean-inspired menu, focusing on fresh, sustainable ingredients. The ambiance is relaxed yet sophisticated, with floor-to-ceiling windows that overlook the pool. Dishes such as the lamb tagine and the butternut squash risotto showcase the restaurant's flair for combining local produce with bold international flavors.

Cuisine: Mediterranean-inspired with an emphasis on sustainable, seasonal ingredients.
Sweetness: Their signature dessert, a light lemon posset with fresh berries, offers a sweet, tangy, and creamy end to your meal.

Bristol offers a broad spectrum of dining experiences to suit every budget and taste. From cozy cafés serving traditional British breakfast staples to luxurious restaurants showcasing the finest seasonal ingredients, there's no shortage of culinary adventures. Whether you're looking for budget-friendly bites, mid-range indulgences, or high-end fine dining, Bristol's diverse food scene promises a memorable meal for every occasion.

Drinks and Desserts Unique to Bristol

Bristol is a city that takes pride in its local produce, creative cuisine, and vibrant food culture. Along with its impressive range of savory dishes, the city also offers some exceptional drinks and desserts that reflect its rich heritage and innovative spirit. Here's a list of drinks and desserts unique to Bristol, each worth trying on your visit:

1. Bristol Cream Sherry

Where to Get It: Available at various pubs and cocktail bars throughout the city, including The Bristol Bar and The Spiny Lobster.
Overview:
While Sherry originated in Spain, Bristol has a long history with this iconic drink, especially with the well-known Bristol Cream Sherry. Known for its sweet and rich taste, Bristol Cream Sherry is a fortified wine that is often served chilled as an aperitif. The drink is smooth with hints of caramel, almonds, and dried fruit. It has become a local favorite, often enjoyed during festive occasions or as a pre-dinner drink.

Cost: Typically £4 - £6 for a glass
Sweetness: This drink has a rich, sweet flavor, balancing the warmth of alcohol with creamy notes and a slightly nutty finish.

2. The Bristol Sour

Where to Get It: Found at many of the city's best cocktail bars, including Hyde & Co. and The Milk Thistle.
Overview:
The Bristol Sour is a modern cocktail that blends the classic Whiskey Sour with a local twist. This drink typically combines whiskey with fresh lemon juice, a touch of sugar syrup, and a unique addition of Bristol Cream Sherry or a local cider brand. The resulting flavor profile is a smooth, slightly tangy, and refreshing drink with a sweet finish from the sherry.

Cost: Around £8 - £12 per cocktail
Sweetness: The drink has a perfect balance between tart citrus and smooth, rich sweetness, making it an enjoyable and balanced cocktail.

3. Bristol Cider

Where to Get It: Available at local cider houses, such as the Bristol Cider Shop and The Apple, a cider bar located on the harbourside.
Overview:
Cider is a significant part of Bristol's identity, and the city boasts a wide selection of craft ciders made from local apples. Bristol Cider comes in a variety of styles, from dry to sweet, sparkling to still. Local cider makers like "Bristol Beer Factory" and "Westons" produce some of the best and most unique ciders in the region. Whether you prefer a traditional apple cider or an innovative fruit-infused option, the cider scene in Bristol is a must-experience.

Cost: £3 - £5 per pint
Sweetness: The sweetness level can vary significantly, from very dry to sweet and fruity, depending on the type of cider you choose.

4. Clotted Cream Ice Cream

Where to Get It: Available at local ice cream parlors such as Marshfield Farm Ice Cream (located just outside Bristol) and The Parlour in Clifton.
Overview:
Clotted Cream Ice Cream is a local delicacy in Bristol, made with the thick, creamy texture of clotted cream that the West Country is famous for. It's rich, indulgent, and smooth, offering a unique twist on traditional ice cream. Often served on its own or paired with a variety of toppings such as fresh berries, chocolate shavings, or caramel sauce, it's a sweet treat that will transport you straight into the heart of Bristol's dairy culture.

Cost: £3 - £5 per scoop
Sweetness: The ice cream is creamy and sweet, with a velvety

smooth texture that makes each bite incredibly satisfying.

5. Bristol Sticky Toffee Pudding

Where to Get It: This classic dessert can be found in many local restaurants and pubs, such as The White Lion and The Pump House.
Overview:
Sticky Toffee Pudding is a beloved dessert in Bristol and throughout the UK. It's a warm, moist sponge cake made with dates, drenched in a rich toffee sauce, and often served with a dollop of clotted cream or a scoop of vanilla ice cream. The dessert is the perfect end to a hearty meal, with its comforting and indulgent sweetness.

Cost: £5 - £8 per portion
Sweetness: As the name suggests, this dessert is incredibly sweet, with deep caramelized flavors and a sticky, toffee-like sauce that oozes over the cake.

6. Bristol Custard Tart

Where to Get It: Often available at local bakeries and cafés such as The Bristol Loaf or Hart's Bakery.
Overview:
The Bristol Custard Tart is a variation of the traditional British custard tart, with a regional twist. This dessert features a buttery, flaky pastry filled with a creamy, smooth custard. The tart is often topped with a light dusting of nutmeg, which gives it a warm and aromatic fragrance. The Bristol version is particularly known for its custard, which is rich but not overly sweet, creating a perfect balance of flavors.

Cost: £2 - £4 per tart
Sweetness: The custard filling is gently sweet and creamy, with a slight hint of vanilla and nutmeg that brings out the dessert's delicate flavors.

7. Apple Cake

Where to Get It: Found in various cafés and bakeries across the city, such as The Cake Shop and The Bristol Food Co-op.
Overview:
Apple Cake is a traditional dessert in the West Country, made with local apples and a light, moist sponge. Often spiced with cinnamon and nutmeg, it brings out the natural sweetness of the apples. This cake is perfect for an afternoon snack or a light dessert, and its comforting flavor makes it a true reflection of the West Country's agricultural roots.

Cost: £3 - £5 per slice
Sweetness: The sweetness comes from the natural apples, with a gentle spiciness from the cinnamon and nutmeg, making it a comforting and subtly sweet treat.

8. Bristolian Donuts

Where to Get It: These locally famous donuts can be found at The Bristolian Café and a few other local food markets such as St. Nicholas Market.
Overview:
The Bristolian Donut is a delicious, deep-fried treat that is filled with cream and dusted with sugar. These soft, fluffy donuts are often filled with a variety of flavors, including vanilla custard, chocolate cream, and jam. They are a popular snack in Bristol, often served fresh and hot, making them perfect for a quick indulgence while exploring the city.

Cost: £2 - £4 per donut
Sweetness: These donuts are sweet, indulgent, and lightly crispy on the outside, with a rich, creamy filling that makes each bite decadent.

TRANSPORTATION

Getting to Bristol: Air, Rail, and Road Options

Bristol, a dynamic and vibrant city located in the heart of the West Country, is well-connected to various transportation hubs across the UK and beyond. Whether you're arriving by air, rail, or road, getting to Bristol is a seamless experience, thanks to its well-established travel infrastructure. Here's a detailed guide to the best ways to reach this exciting city:

1. By Air: Bristol Airport

Location: Bristol Airport (BRS) is located approximately 8 miles southwest of the city center, near the village of Lulsgate Bottom.
Travel Time to City Center: 25 minutes by car or taxi, and approximately 30-40 minutes by public transport.
Overview:
Bristol Airport serves as the primary gateway for international and domestic travelers visiting the city. It is a modern, well-equipped airport offering a range of flights from major cities in Europe and beyond. The airport handles both budget airlines and full-service carriers, making it accessible for various budgets. It serves destinations across Europe, including Spain, France, Germany, Italy,

and Ireland, as well as more distant locations like Turkey, Dubai, and the Canary Islands.

Upon arrival, travelers can easily access the city center via various transportation options. The airport is well-connected by bus, coach, and taxi services, with frequent direct routes to and from Bristol city center and other key locations, such as Bath, Cardiff, and London.

How to Get There:

- **Bus & Coach:** Bristol Airport is well-served by several public transportation options, including the Bristol Airport Flyer Express Bus, which connects the airport with Temple Meads Railway Station and the city center. Coaches from National Express and Megabus also offer services to other cities, such as London and Birmingham.
- **Taxis and Ride-Sharing:** Taxis are readily available at the airport, and services like Uber are also popular for a more personalized experience.

Airlines:

- EasyJet
- Ryanair
- Wizz Air
- KLM
- TUI Airways

2. By Rail: Bristol Temple Meads Station

Location: Bristol Temple Meads Railway Station is situated about 1 mile from the city center, with easy access to local attractions, hotels, and amenities.

Travel Time to City Center: 5-10 minutes by foot, or a short taxi ride if you prefer.

Overview:
Bristol Temple Meads is the city's main railway station and one of the busiest in the UK, connecting Bristol to major cities across the country. The station, with its historical architecture and modern

facilities, is a central hub for regional, intercity, and high-speed rail services.

Travelers arriving by train can choose from a range of direct routes from cities such as London, Cardiff, Birmingham, Exeter, and Manchester. Trains to and from Bristol are operated by Great Western Railway, CrossCountry, and other regional services. Bristol's location on the main line between London and the southwest makes it an easy destination to access from most parts of the UK.

Notable Routes:

- **London to Bristol:** The journey from London Paddington to Bristol takes around 1 hour 45 minutes on a direct train. High-speed services operate regularly throughout the day.
- **Cardiff to Bristol:** The direct journey between Cardiff and Bristol takes approximately 45 minutes, with trains running frequently throughout the day.
- **Manchester to Bristol:** Direct trains between Manchester and Bristol typically take around 3 hours.

How to Get There:

- **Buses & Local Transport:** From the station, visitors can catch local buses, taxis, or walk into the heart of the city. There are several bus stops near Temple Meads with routes to various parts of Bristol.

3. By Road: Driving and Bus Services

Location and Overview:
Bristol is easily accessible by road, with convenient connections to the M4, M5, and M32 motorways. Whether you are driving yourself or taking a coach, getting to Bristol by road offers a smooth journey, with a range of services and routes available from surrounding cities and beyond.

- **M4 Motorway:** The M4 connects London and the South East

to Bristol, making it one of the fastest routes for those traveling from the capital. The journey takes approximately 2 hours by car.
- **M5 Motorway:** For those coming from the South West, the M5 is a direct route into Bristol, passing through cities such as Exeter and Taunton. It provides easy access from Cornwall, Devon, and the Midlands.
- **M32 Motorway:** The M32 connects Bristol to the M4, bringing you directly into the city center. It's the most direct route for those coming from the east.

Driving in Bristol:
While Bristol is well-connected by road, it's worth noting that the city center can get busy, particularly during rush hours. Parking in the city center is available, but it can be expensive, especially in the more tourist-heavy areas. It's advisable to book parking in advance if you're driving.

Bus and Coach Services:
Bristol is also served by extensive bus and coach services that offer affordable travel options for those coming from other parts of the UK. National Express and Megabus operate regular services from London, Cardiff, Birmingham, and other major cities.

- **National Express:** Offers direct coach routes from major UK cities, including London, Birmingham, and Manchester, to Bristol.
- **Megabus:** Budget-friendly services run frequently from cities such as London, Birmingham, and Cardiff, with fares starting as low as £1.

No matter how you choose to travel, Bristol is easily accessible by air, rail, or road. Its excellent transport links make it a perfect city to visit for both short getaways and longer stays. With Bristol Airport offering a range of international and domestic flights, and its major railway station providing convenient access to cities across the UK, getting to Bristol has never been easier. For those traveling by road, the city's extensive motorway network makes it straightforward to reach from most regions of the UK. Once you're in Bristol, getting around is equally simple, with excellent local public transport services ensuring you can navigate the city with ease.

Navigating the City: Public Transportation Tips

Bristol, with its bustling streets, vibrant neighborhoods, and stunning riverside views, is a city that's a joy to explore. Thankfully, getting around is made easy by a well-developed and efficient public transportation system. Whether you're commuting to work, exploring attractions, or simply enjoying the city's charms, there are a variety of options at your disposal. Here's a guide to help you navigate the city like a local.

1. Buses: The Backbone of Bristol's Public Transport

Overview:
 Bristol's bus network is extensive, covering all parts of the city and beyond, making it one of the most popular ways to get around. The bus system is run by First Bus, which operates a range of routes connecting key areas within the city, as well as destinations further afield, such as Bath, Weston-super-Mare, and even the countryside.

Key Features:

- **Coverage:** The bus system covers all major neighborhoods, including Clifton, Bedminster, Stokes Croft, and more. Buses frequently stop near popular attractions, shopping districts, and dining spots.
- **Frequency:** Buses run regularly throughout the day, with the frequency varying depending on the time of day. During peak hours, buses can arrive every 5 to 10 minutes. Late-night services are available, though with reduced frequencies.
- **Tickets:** Tickets can be purchased from the bus driver

directly or via the First Bus app, which also allows you to track buses in real-time. You can opt for a single journey ticket or a day pass, which offers unlimited travel for a set number of hours.

Tips:

- **Planning Your Journey:** The First Bus app is your best friend for planning bus trips, offering live timetables and real-time tracking.
- **Bus Routes:** The number 8, 9, and 24 are particularly useful for tourists, connecting major sites like the Clifton Suspension Bridge, Bristol Museum & Art Gallery, and Bristol Harbourside.
- **Sustainable Travel:** Consider opting for the Bristol's Green Travel schemes, such as the "U-Bus" service, which features electric buses, making for an eco-friendly travel option.

2. Trams: A Newer Mode of Transport

Overview:

Bristol's tram system is a relatively new addition to its public transportation landscape but has quickly become a popular and scenic way to get around. The MetroBus service is Bristol's answer to modern light rail systems, providing a rapid and efficient link between key areas, including the city center, Temple Meads, and the airport.

Key Features:

- **MetroBus Routes:** MetroBus operates several lines that connect to major hubs, including the A4 route from Bristol Airport to the city center. It's fast, efficient, and a convenient way to bypass the city's congested streets.
- **Comfort & Accessibility:** Trams are spacious and accessible, with low floors for easy access for people with disabilities. They also come equipped with Wi-Fi and air conditioning for added comfort.

- **Ticketing:** You can purchase tickets directly from the driver or use the MetroBus app, which allows you to plan your journey and view real-time schedules.

Tips:

- **Sights Along the Way:** The MetroBus routes offer a glimpse of Bristol's varied landscapes. Take a ride from the airport into the city center to get a scenic view of the countryside and Bristol's iconic architecture.
- **Avoiding Traffic:** Since the tram routes are often dedicated to buses and trams, they're a great way to avoid the city's notorious traffic jams.

3. Cycling: A Green and Active Option

Overview:
Bristol is a cyclist's paradise, and many locals and tourists alike take advantage of the city's excellent cycling infrastructure. With dedicated bike lanes, bike hire schemes, and a commitment to green travel, cycling is a fantastic way to explore Bristol's neighborhoods at your own pace.

Key Features:

- **Bristol's Cycling Network:** The city has invested heavily in bike lanes and bike-friendly roads, making cycling safe and convenient. Key routes include those along the harborside, through Queen Square, and across the iconic Clifton Suspension Bridge.
- **Bike Hire:** For those who don't bring their own bikes, Bristol has a range of bike hire services, including the "YoBike" scheme, where you can rent and drop off bikes at designated locations across the city.
- **Sustainability:** Cycling in Bristol isn't just practical; it's also a sustainable way to travel. With increasing efforts towards reducing carbon emissions, cycling helps you make a positive impact on the environment.

Tips:

- **Cycle-Friendly Routes:** One of the best ways to explore Bristol is by bike. The Harbourside and the River Avon towpath offer scenic and mostly flat routes, perfect for leisurely cycling.
- **Safety First:** Always wear a helmet and ensure that your bike is properly secured if you're leaving it unattended.

4. Walking: A City Best Explored on Foot

Overview:

While Bristol offers various modes of transport, one of the best ways to experience the city is on foot. Bristol's compact city center makes it easy to walk between major attractions, trendy neighborhoods, and picturesque spots.

Key Features:

- **Walkable City Center:** Bristol is a highly walkable city, with its historical architecture, charming cobbled streets, and scenic riverbanks all easily accessible on foot. Key attractions like the Clifton Suspension Bridge, Bristol Cathedral, and St. Nicholas Market are all within walking distance from the city center.
- **Walking Tours:** If you want to delve deeper into the city's history, you can take a guided walking tour. These tours often include fascinating facts about Bristol's maritime heritage, street art culture, and local history.

Tips:

- **Explore Hidden Gems:** Bristol is known for its hidden gems – quirky shops, secret gardens, and local cafes – that are best discovered on foot. Wander down side streets and alleyways for unexpected treasures.
- **Wear Comfortable Shoes:** With so much to see and do, comfortable walking shoes are a must to enjoy your Bristol adventure without any discomfort.

5. Taxis & Ride-Hailing Services: Convenience at Your Doorstep

Overview:
For those who prefer a more direct and private way of getting around, taxis and ride-hailing services like Uber are readily available throughout the city. Whether you're heading to the airport, exploring further afield, or simply need to get home after a night out, these services provide a door-to-door solution.

Key Features:

- **Taxi Services:** Bristol is home to a large fleet of licensed black cabs and private hire vehicles. Taxis can be hailed on the street or booked in advance. Many taxis are also accessible for people with disabilities.
- **Ride-Hailing:** Services like Uber are also widely available, offering the convenience of booking a ride directly from your phone. The app lets you track your ride, see fare estimates, and rate your driver.

Tips:

- **Peak Times:** Taxis and ride-hailing services can be busy during rush hour or when there are major events in the city, so it's always a good idea to plan ahead if you need a ride at these times.
- **Cost:** Taxis typically have a minimum fare, with charges increasing based on distance. Ride-hailing fares are variable, but often more affordable than traditional taxis, especially for short trips.

Bristol is a city that's both accessible and enjoyable to explore through its public transport system. With buses, trams, cycling options, and walking routes, you'll find getting around easy and convenient. Whether you're navigating the streets for business, leisure, or adventure, these options give you the freedom to explore the city's diverse districts, stunning views, and cultural heritage. To make the most of your time, plan your journeys ahead, consider sustainable options, and enjoy the city from every angle!

Bike and Scooter Rentals: Eco-Friendly Travel

Bristol is known for its vibrant culture, picturesque streets, and commitment to sustainability, making it the perfect city to explore on two wheels. Whether you're zipping around the city center or cruising along the scenic riverbanks, bike and scooter rentals offer a flexible and eco-friendly way to get around. This sustainable transportation option not only helps reduce the city's carbon footprint but also gives you the chance to enjoy Bristol's charm at your own pace. Here's a closer look at bike and scooter rentals in Bristol and how to make the most of this green travel option.

1. Bike Rentals: Pedal Your Way Around Bristol

Overview:
Bristol is one of the UK's most bike-friendly cities, with an extensive network of cycling lanes, quiet streets, and cycling-friendly infrastructure. For those looking to travel sustainably, bike rentals are a great option. The city offers several bike-sharing schemes, allowing both locals and tourists to rent bikes easily and explore the city's attractions.

Key Features:

- **YoBike:** YoBike is one of the most popular bike-sharing services in Bristol. With YoBike, you can rent a bike through their app, pick it up from any station, and drop it off at a designated bike station. The bikes are brightly colored and easily spotted around the city.
- **Public Bike Stands:** You'll find bike racks across the city at key locations, making it convenient to pick up or drop off bikes. The rental process is straightforward, and the bikes are designed for short trips around town.

- **Eco-Friendly:** Renting a bike is a sustainable way to travel. Bristol has invested heavily in creating bike lanes and paths, making it safer and more convenient to cycle.

Pricing:

- **YoBike Pricing:** YoBike offers a flexible pay-as-you-go model, with rates typically starting at £1 for a 30-minute ride. Discounts are available for longer trips or memberships, making it an affordable and environmentally friendly travel option.

Tips:

- **Cycle-Friendly Routes:** Take advantage of Bristol's many dedicated bike lanes, including those along the Harbourside and the River Avon, for a scenic ride through the city.
- **Safety First:** Make sure to wear a helmet (available to buy or rent at bike stations) and follow road safety rules. Keep an eye out for traffic, especially when riding on busier roads.

2. Scooter Rentals: A Fun and Fast Way to Explore

Overview:
For those who prefer a little more speed, scooter rentals are an increasingly popular choice in Bristol. These electric scooters are a fun and efficient way to explore the city without breaking a sweat. With their eco-friendly design and ease of use, scooters are perfect for both short trips around the city and longer excursions to explore different neighborhoods.

Key Features:

- **Voi Scooters:** Voi is a popular electric scooter rental service in Bristol, offering a convenient, app-based way to rent scooters throughout the city. Once you download the Voi app, you can locate nearby scooters, unlock them with your phone, and start your ride. The scooters are designed for urban commuting, featuring comfortable grips and smooth

acceleration.
- **Availability:** Scooters are available in several key areas of Bristol, including the city center, Temple Meads, and along the waterfront. You'll find designated scooter parking zones throughout the city.
- **Eco-Friendly:** By using electric scooters, you can reduce your carbon footprint and help keep the city's air clean. The scooters are powered by rechargeable batteries, making them an environmentally responsible alternative to traditional vehicles.

Pricing:

- **Voi Pricing:** Voi's pricing structure is typically around £1 to unlock the scooter, with an additional charge of around 20p per minute for use. This makes scooters an affordable and convenient mode of transportation, especially for short trips around the city.
- **Discounts:** Voi also offers discounted rates for students, frequent riders, or those who use scooters for commuting, making it an even more cost-effective choice.

Tips:

- **Safety Gear:** While helmets aren't provided by the scooter rental services, it's a good idea to bring your own or purchase one from a nearby store. Riding safely is crucial, so always wear protective gear when available.
- **Scooter Etiquette:** When riding a scooter, always be mindful of pedestrians, cyclists, and other road users. Stick to bike lanes where possible, and park your scooter in designated areas to avoid blocking walkways.

Benefits of Bike and Scooter Rentals in Bristol

- **Sustainability:** Both bike and scooter rentals provide an eco-friendly alternative to car travel, helping reduce traffic congestion and air pollution in the city.

- **Convenience:** With rental stations spread across the city, you can easily find a bike or scooter near your location, making it convenient to explore attractions or quickly get from one place to another.
- **Health Benefits:** Cycling and scootering provide low-impact exercise, allowing you to stay active while exploring the city in an enjoyable way.
- **Affordability:** Renting a bike or scooter is often cheaper than taking a taxi or public transport, making it an ideal option for budget-conscious travelers.

Whether you're pedaling through the streets or cruising on an electric scooter, renting a bike or scooter in Bristol offers a fun and sustainable way to experience the city. With affordable prices, easy access, and eco-friendly benefits, these options are perfect for anyone wanting to explore Bristol while minimizing their environmental impact. So, grab a bike or scooter, and start your adventure through this beautiful, green city!

Taxi and Ride-Share Costs

Bristol offers a variety of transportation options for those who prefer the convenience of door-to-door service. Whether you're arriving from the airport, heading out for a night in the city, or simply need to get from point A to point B, taxis and ride-share services are readily available. Understanding the cost structures of these services will help you plan your transportation budget while in the city.

1. Traditional Taxis: A Convenient Choice

Overview:
 Traditional black cabs are a common sight in Bristol, offering a comfortable and reliable means of transport around the city. Taxis are licensed by the local council, and passengers can hail a taxi on the street, book one via phone, or find them at designated taxi ranks across the city, such as near train stations or shopping areas. Taxis

in Bristol are a great option for those who want to avoid the hassle of navigating public transport or prefer a more direct route.

Costs:

- **Starting Fare:** The base fare for a taxi ride in Bristol typically starts at around £3.20 for the first mile, with additional charges depending on the distance traveled.
- **Per Mile Rate:** After the first mile, taxis charge around £1.80 to £2.00 per mile.
- **Additional Charges:** There may be extra charges for luggage, waiting time, or late-night rides, with some taxis adding a surcharge between 11 PM and 6 AM.

For example, a 5-mile journey in the city would likely cost between £12 and £15, depending on traffic and the time of day.

Tips:

- **Booking in Advance:** While taxis can be hailed from the street, it's often more reliable to book one in advance, especially during peak times like rush hour or on weekends.
- **Taxi Ranks:** Look out for taxi ranks around the city's main transport hubs, such as Bristol Temple Meads Station, where you'll find a number of taxis waiting for passengers.

2. Ride-Share Services: Flexibility and Convenience

Overview:
For a modern alternative to traditional taxis, ride-share services like Uber, Bolt, and Ola are widely available in Bristol. These apps offer an easy and convenient way to book a ride directly from your phone, with the ability to track your driver's arrival in real-time. Ride-sharing services are generally known for their competitive pricing, ease of use, and the ability to choose from different types of vehicles (economy, luxury, or larger cars for groups).

Costs:

- **Base Fare:** Ride-share services usually start with a base fare of approximately £1.50 to £2.00. This is similar to the starting fare of a traditional taxi.
- **Per Mile Rate:** The per-mile cost varies by the ride-sharing platform and the car type. For example, with Uber, the cost per mile is approximately £1.00 to £1.30, depending on demand.
- **Surge Pricing:** One important consideration when using ride-share services is surge pricing, which can significantly increase costs during busy periods, such as Friday evenings or during events. During surge pricing, rates can sometimes be up to 2-3 times higher than the normal fare.

For example, a 5-mile ride during peak hours might cost between £12 and £18, while off-peak travel might result in a cost closer to £9-£12.

Tips:

- **Check the App for Fares:** Always check the fare estimate before confirming your ride. Apps like Uber provide a fare estimate based on current traffic and demand.
- **Avoid Surge Pricing:** If you can wait a few minutes or travel during non-peak hours, you can save money by avoiding surge pricing, which is often triggered during peak demand times.
- **Ride Options:** Different platforms offer various vehicle options. If you're traveling solo, you can opt for the standard ride; for larger groups, you might consider an XL or family-sized vehicle.

3. Comparison of Taxi vs. Ride-Share

When choosing between a traditional taxi and a ride-share service in Bristol, it often comes down to convenience, cost, and personal preference. Here's a quick comparison:

Feature	Traditional Taxis	Ride-Share Services (e.g., Uber, Bolt)
Availability	Available from taxi ranks or via phone booking	Available via app, quick booking
Pricing	Starts at £3.20, £1.80 per mile after that	Starts at £1.50-£2, £1.00-£1.30 per mile
Surge Pricing	No surge pricing	Surge pricing can increase fares during high demand
Payment Methods	Cash or card	Credit/debit card via the app
Booking Process	Hail or call for a cab	Book via smartphone app

Taxi services in Bristol are a great option if you prefer a traditional and reliable form of transportation. However, ride-share services like Uber and Bolt are often more convenient and affordable, especially for short trips or when traveling during non-peak hours. Understanding both options will help you make the most informed choice based on your travel needs and budget. Whether you choose a traditional cab or a modern ride-share, both offer comfort and flexibility for getting around the city.

PRACTICAL ADVICE

Safety Tips for Travelers

Bristol is a vibrant and welcoming city, renowned for its rich history, stunning landmarks, and lively cultural scene. However, like any major city, it's important to stay aware of your surroundings and take precautions to ensure your safety. Whether you're exploring the city on foot, traveling by public transport, or enjoying the local nightlife, here are some essential safety tips to keep in mind during your visit to Bristol.

1. Keep Your Belongings Secure

Overview:
As with most bustling cities, keeping your belongings secure should always be a top priority. Bristol is generally safe, but it's still essential to stay vigilant, particularly in busy areas like shopping streets, markets, and tourist attractions.

Tips:

- **Use Anti-Theft Bags:** Consider using a crossbody bag with a zipper or an anti-theft backpack that has hidden zippers and straps, making it harder for pickpockets to access your belongings.

- **Keep Valuables Hidden:** Avoid flaunting expensive gadgets, jewelry, or large sums of cash, especially in crowded areas or on public transport.
- **Be Cautious in Crowded Places:** Pickpockets often target crowded areas such as public transport stations or popular attractions like Clifton Suspension Bridge. Always be mindful of your surroundings.

2. Use Reputable Transport Services

Overview:
Getting around Bristol is relatively easy, but ensuring that you're using trusted transportation services is key to staying safe.

Tips:

- **Use Licensed Taxis and Ride Shares:** When using a taxi or ride-share service (such as Uber), always ensure it is licensed. For taxis, look for the official city registration badge. With ride-sharing apps, check the vehicle details and driver information before getting in.
- **Avoid Strangers Offering Unsolicited Rides:** While it's tempting to take up offers from friendly locals, avoid accepting rides from unlicensed or unofficial transport providers. Stick to taxis, buses, or ride-share apps.
- **Stay Alert at Night:** If traveling at night, try to use well-lit and populated streets. When using public transportation after dark, be cautious and sit in more visible, well-trafficked carriages or buses.

3. Be Cautious in the Nightlife Scene

Overview:
Bristol has an exciting nightlife scene with bars, clubs, and live music venues spread across the city. While it's a great way to experience the city's culture, it's important to be cautious when enjoying the night out.

Tips:

- **Stay with Friends:** It's always safer to explore Bristol's nightlife in groups, especially if you're unfamiliar with the city. Keep an eye on your belongings and watch out for each other.
- **Drink Responsibly:** While Bristol's pubs and bars offer delicious local craft beers and cocktails, always drink responsibly. Make sure to never leave your drink unattended or accept drinks from strangers.
- **Know Your Route Home:** Plan your route back to your accommodation in advance, whether it's via public transport, taxi, or a ride-share service. If walking home, try to stick to well-lit areas and avoid shortcuts through poorly lit parks or alleys.

4. Emergency Contacts and Services

Overview:
Although Bristol is a relatively safe city, emergencies can still happen. Knowing the key emergency contacts and how to reach help in the event of an incident is vital for peace of mind.

Tips:

- **Emergency Number:** The UK's emergency number is **999**, which connects you to police, ambulance, or fire services.
- **Nearest Hospital:** The **Bristol Royal Infirmary (BRI)** is one of the city's major hospitals and is easily accessible from most parts of the city center.
- **Travel Insurance:** It's advisable to have travel insurance that covers medical emergencies, lost luggage, or cancellations, giving you a safety net in case of unforeseen circumstances.

5. Stay Informed About Weather Conditions

Overview:
Bristol's weather can be unpredictable, with occasional rainfall,

even in summer months. Being prepared for the weather is an essential part of staying safe during your trip.

Tips:

- **Check the Weather Forecast:** Before heading out, especially for outdoor activities like walking tours or hiking, check the weather forecast to prepare accordingly.
- **Carry an Umbrella or Raincoat:** Having a small, foldable umbrella or a lightweight rain jacket can help protect you from sudden showers.
- **Dress in Layers:** The temperature can fluctuate throughout the day, so layering your clothes will keep you comfortable as you move through the city.

6. Be Mindful of Traffic

Overview:
While Bristol is a pedestrian-friendly city, traffic can still be heavy in certain areas, particularly during rush hour. Being cautious around traffic is important for your safety.

Tips:

- **Use Crosswalks:** Always use pedestrian crossings and wait for the signal to cross roads. Avoid jaywalking, especially in busy streets and intersections.
- **Look Both Ways:** Even on quieter streets, always look both ways before crossing. Watch out for cyclists and buses, which may be harder to notice due to their size.
- **Cycling Safety:** If you're cycling in Bristol, ensure you're wearing a helmet and follow traffic rules. The city has bike lanes in several parts, but cyclists should still stay aware of the traffic around them.

7. Personal Safety in Unfamiliar Areas

Overview:
Bristol is generally a safe city, but some areas may be quieter or less populated than others. It's important to exercise extra caution if you're exploring unfamiliar neighborhoods, especially at night.

Tips:

- **Stick to Well-Lit Areas at Night:** When walking around in the evenings, avoid poorly lit streets and isolated areas. Opt for main roads and busy thoroughfares that have foot traffic.
- **Know Your Surroundings:** Familiarize yourself with your accommodation's location and local landmarks. Using maps or GPS on your phone can be helpful if you're unsure of your surroundings.
- **Ask Locals for Advice:** Don't hesitate to ask locals for advice on areas to avoid or for tips on safe routes around the city. Bristol residents are often friendly and willing to assist travelers.

By following these safety tips, you'll be able to make the most of your trip to Bristol while feeling confident and secure. Always stay alert, respect the local customs, and take the necessary precautions when exploring new places. With safety as your priority, Bristol's charm, history, and vibrant atmosphere will be there for you to enjoy.

Language and Communication in Bristol

Bristol is a vibrant, multicultural city where English is the primary language spoken. However, like many cities in the UK, Bristol is home to a wide variety of accents, dialects, and languages, which gives the city its unique character and flavor. Whether you're visiting as a tourist, relocating for work, or simply passing through, understanding the language and communication norms will enhance your experience and help you navigate the city with ease.

1. English: The Primary Language

Overview:
English is the primary language spoken in Bristol, and most interactions, whether at restaurants, hotels, tourist attractions, or on public transport, will be conducted in English. The dialect of English spoken in Bristol is commonly referred to as "Bristolian" and has its own unique charm. While it may sound distinct, it's still based on standard British English.

Key Points:

- **Accent:** The Bristol accent, which can sometimes be strong, is known for its distinctive "r" sound and its unique pronunciation of vowels. It's part of the West Country dialect, which is also common in surrounding areas like Somerset and Cornwall.
- **Local Phrases:** While most visitors will have no trouble understanding standard English, you might hear some local phrases and colloquialisms. For instance, "gert lush" means something is really good or impressive, and "chopsy" can describe someone who is outspoken or cheeky.
- **Communication Style:** Bristol's residents tend to be friendly and approachable. They're known for their down-to-earth, open demeanor, so don't hesitate to strike up a conversation or ask for directions. People in Bristol are generally very helpful to visitors.

2. Regional Dialects and Accents

Overview:
As you explore the city, you may notice that Bristolians have a distinctive regional accent, known as the Bristolian accent, which differs from other parts of the UK. Understanding a few of the common words and phrases can help you feel more at ease in conversations.

Key Points:

- **Bristolian Phrases:** Some popular phrases that you might come across include "You alright?" (which is equivalent to "How are you?") and "I'm off down the shops" (meaning "I'm going to the store").
- **Rhotic Accent:** In Bristol, the "r" sound is more pronounced than in many other parts of England, giving the accent a unique texture. For instance, "car" might sound more like "cah," with a pronounced roll of the 'r' at the end.
- **Don't Worry About Misunderstandings:** While Bristolian is distinctive, it is generally very understandable, and people are often more than happy to slow down or clarify if you're unfamiliar with the local accent.

3. Multicultural Influence: Languages Spoken in Bristol

Overview:
Bristol is a diverse city, and you'll likely encounter a range of languages being spoken throughout the city, particularly in areas like St. Paul's, Easton, and the city center. These neighborhoods reflect the city's multicultural community, with a significant number of residents hailing from countries around the world.

Key Points:

- **Common Languages:** Apart from English, some of the most common languages spoken in Bristol include Somali, Polish, Portuguese, Arabic, and Punjabi. Depending on where you are in the city, you might hear these languages in shops, restaurants, or cultural hubs.
- **Bristol's Vibrant Communities:** The multicultural makeup of Bristol is part of what gives the city its energy. You'll encounter diverse cultures through food, festivals, and events. For example, the St. Paul's Carnival celebrates Afro-Caribbean culture, and the Bristol Somali Week showcases the city's Somali heritage.
- **Learning Key Phrases:** While English is dominant, learning a few basic words in another language (like "hello" or "thank

you") can be a nice gesture of respect for the local communities.

4. British Etiquette and Communication Norms

Overview:
When communicating in Bristol, it's helpful to understand British social norms and etiquette. Bristolians, like most Brits, tend to value politeness, understatement, and indirectness. Being aware of these can make your interactions smoother and more pleasant.

Key Points:

- **Politeness is Key:** Saying "please" and "thank you" is essential in almost every interaction. Whether you're asking for directions or ordering food, using these words shows respect and politeness.
- **Personal Space:** Britons generally value personal space, and it's important to maintain a comfortable distance during conversations, especially with strangers.
- **Making Small Talk:** Brits are known for their love of small talk, which often revolves around neutral subjects like the weather, sports, or current events. It's an excellent icebreaker and can be a good way to start a conversation with a local.
- **Indirect Communication:** In some situations, people may not be as direct as in other cultures. For example, a British person may say "I'm not sure about that," when they actually mean "No," or "It might be possible," when they mean "No." Learning to read between the lines is an important communication skill.

5. Communication in the Digital Age: Using Technology in Bristol

Overview:

In today's connected world, many travelers rely on smartphones and digital apps to communicate and navigate cities. In Bristol, you'll find that digital communication is just as important as face-to-face interaction, whether it's for ordering food, getting directions, or understanding public transport systems.

Key Points:

- **Smartphones and Apps:** Wi-Fi is widely available in cafes, restaurants, and public spaces around the city. Apps like Google Translate, CityMapper, and Uber can help you get around or communicate if you're not familiar with the language or transit system.
- **Social Media:** Bristol is an active city on social media, and you'll often find local businesses, cultural events, and community groups interacting with residents and visitors alike. Follow hashtags like #BristolLife or #VisitBristol to keep up with the latest events and trends.
- **Mobile Numbers and SIM Cards:** If you're staying for an extended period and need to stay connected, consider purchasing a UK SIM card. Local stores like WHSmith or supermarkets like Tesco offer pay-as-you-go SIM cards with competitive data packages.

6. Accessibility for Non-English Speakers

Overview:
Bristol is a very tourist-friendly city, and while English is predominant, the local tourism industry is well-equipped to assist non-English speakers. Many popular attractions, restaurants, and transport services offer assistance in multiple languages.

Key Points:

- **Multilingual Signage:** Many public transport systems, museums, and tourist sites offer multilingual signage to help international visitors. This is particularly useful for people

who are unfamiliar with English or the city's layout.
- **Language Assistance at Tourist Centers:** Bristol's Visitor Information Centres can provide assistance to non-English speakers, and staff may be able to help with translations or guide you to English-speaking services.

Bristol's linguistic landscape is rich and diverse, with English being the main language but accompanied by a mix of accents, dialects, and languages from around the world. Understanding the local dialects, being aware of British etiquette, and making use of technology will ensure you have a smooth and enjoyable experience when communicating in the city. Whether you're exploring Bristol's neighborhoods or engaging with the friendly locals, embracing the city's linguistic diversity will enhance your stay and make your visit even more memorable.

Emergency Contacts and Services in Bristol

When traveling to a new city, it's crucial to familiarize yourself with local emergency services and contacts. Whether you find yourself in need of urgent medical assistance, a police response, or any other emergency situation, knowing who to contact and how to reach help quickly can ensure your safety and peace of mind. Bristol, like other major cities in the UK, offers a range of emergency services that are reliable and easy to access.

1. Emergency Numbers in Bristol

Overview:
 In the UK, emergency services can be reached through a single emergency phone number, ensuring simplicity in urgent situations.

- **Emergency Number (All Services): 999**
  This is the national emergency contact number for police,

fire, ambulance, and other emergency services. Dialing **999** connects you to an operator who will ask which service you require and quickly redirect your call to the appropriate service.

- **Alternative Emergency Number: 112**
  This is the same as 999 and works in the same way. It is commonly used across Europe and works in the UK as well, so you can dial **112** if you're in an emergency situation.

Key Points:

- Both numbers are free of charge and available 24/7.
- You can call these numbers from any phone, including mobile, landline, and payphones.

2. Medical Emergency Services (Ambulance)

Overview:
In the case of medical emergencies or urgent health issues, calling **999** will connect you to an ambulance service. The UK's National Health Service (NHS) provides emergency healthcare, and you will be transported to the nearest hospital or medical facility.

- **NHS Direct (Non-Emergency Medical Advice): 111**
  For non-urgent health concerns, you can call **111** for medical advice, information, or guidance on whether you need to visit a healthcare professional.

Key Points:

- Ambulance services in the UK are available throughout the city, including Bristol, and response times may vary depending on the nature of the emergency.
- For serious or life-threatening situations, an ambulance can reach you quickly after dialing **999**.

3. Police Services

Overview:
The **Avon and Somerset Police** are responsible for law enforcement in Bristol. Whether you're a victim of crime, witness to an incident, or need to report a suspicious activity, the police can provide assistance.

- **Emergency Police Number: 999**
  For immediate emergencies or crimes in progress, call **999** to reach the police quickly.

- **Non-Emergency Police Number: 101**
  If you need to report a crime that is not an emergency (e.g., theft, vandalism), you can reach the police through **101**. This number can also be used to inquire about incidents, services, or ongoing investigations.

Key Points:

- **Police Stations in Bristol:** Several police stations are spread across the city, including **Bristol Central Police Station** located in the city center, which is easily accessible for emergencies.
- For ongoing incidents, or in case of immediate danger, always dial **999** for urgent police assistance.

4. Fire Services

Overview:
The **Avon Fire and Rescue Service** is responsible for fire safety in Bristol. In case of fire, explosion, or rescue-related emergencies, you should immediately contact the fire department.

- **Emergency Fire Number: 999**
  Dial **999** for fires, smoke inhalation, rescue operations, and hazardous material incidents.

Key Points:

- **Fire Safety:** In Bristol, fire safety is a priority, with regular fire drills and well-maintained fire alarms in public buildings. Be sure to follow fire safety guidelines when staying in hotels, apartments, or other accommodations.
- Firefighters are well-equipped to handle a wide range of emergency scenarios, including hazardous material spillages and technical rescues.

5. Nearest Hospitals and Medical Facilities

Overview:
Knowing where the nearest hospitals and medical centers are located can save valuable time in case of a health emergency. Bristol offers several healthcare facilities that provide immediate care and treatment.

- **Bristol Royal Infirmary (BRI)**
  Location: Upper Maudlin St, Bristol BS2 8HW
  Opening Hours: 24/7
  Overview: This major teaching hospital offers a wide range of emergency medical services. It is a renowned facility in the region for treating serious injuries, surgical operations, and intensive care.
  Cost: The NHS covers emergency care; however, if you are visiting from outside the UK, charges may apply depending on your circumstances.

- **St. Michael's Hospital**
  Location: Bristol BS2 8ED
  Opening Hours: 24/7
  Overview: A well-equipped hospital providing emergency care, particularly known for its maternity and women's health services. It also provides 24/7 emergency treatment for minor injuries and illnesses.

- **Southmead Hospital**

Location: Southmead Rd, Westbury-on-Trym, Bristol BS10 5NB
Opening Hours: 24/7
Overview: Southmead Hospital is a large facility providing emergency and trauma care. It is well-staffed and offers specialized care for complex injuries and conditions.

Key Points:

- You will never be turned away from an NHS hospital in an emergency, but you may need to wait depending on the severity of your case.
- If you're a visitor, travel insurance may cover the costs of treatment in the event of a medical emergency.

6. Lost Property

Overview:
In the unfortunate event that you lose something while traveling in Bristol, it's good to know where to report lost items and how to retrieve them.

- **Lost Property Office at Bristol Temple Meads Station**
  Location: Temple Meads, Bristol BS1 6QF
  Opening Hours: Mon-Fri, 8:00 AM - 6:00 PM; Sat-Sun, 9:00 AM - 4:00 PM
  Overview: If you lose any personal belongings on public transport, in taxis, or at the station, this office can assist in retrieving your items.

- **Bristol City Council Lost Property Office**
  Location: City Hall, College Green, Bristol BS1 5TR
  Opening Hours: Mon-Fri, 9:00 AM - 5:00 PM
  Overview: For items lost in public places, parks, or council-managed venues, you can contact the Lost Property Office for assistance.

7. Insurance and Assistance Services

Overview:
Travel insurance is a vital part of preparing for your trip, and it's important to have access to assistance services for any unexpected situations, such as flight cancellations, medical emergencies, or lost luggage.

- **European Health Insurance Card (EHIC):** If you are from an EU country, the **EHIC** can help cover some medical costs during your stay.
- **Travel Insurance Companies:** It's advisable to have travel insurance covering health, theft, or loss of possessions. Most major travel insurance providers offer 24/7 assistance hotlines to help you through emergencies.

When visiting Bristol, it's essential to stay informed about emergency contacts and services, so you're well-prepared for any situation. Whether you need medical assistance, a police report, or fire services, help is just a phone call away. Understanding the procedures and knowing where to find the nearest hospitals, police stations, and lost property offices will give you peace of mind during your trip. Always ensure you have travel insurance and know the emergency numbers for added security.

VISA UPDATES AND ENTRY REQUIREMENTS

How to Apply for a UK Visa: Step-by-Step Guide

Applying for a UK visa, whether it's for tourism, work, study, or any other reason, requires a clear understanding of the process to ensure a smooth experience. The following step-by-step guide will walk you through the entire application process, from gathering necessary documents to submitting your application and attending biometric appointments. This guide is designed to help you navigate the visa application process with confidence, ensuring that you meet all entry requirements for your trip to Bristol, UK.

Step 1: Determine the Type of Visa You Need

Before you begin the application process, it's essential to determine the correct type of visa for your specific travel needs. The UK offers several visa categories, including:

- **Standard Visitor Visa** (for tourism, family visits, or short-term business).
- **Skilled Worker Visa** (for employment in a qualified job).

- **Student Visa** (for studying at a recognized educational institution).
- **Family Visitor Visa** (for visiting family members in the UK).
- **Business Visitor Visa** (for attending meetings, conferences, or conducting business activities).

Visit the official UK government website to review the different types of visas available and choose the one that suits your purpose.

Step 2: Check Eligibility Requirements

Once you have determined the appropriate visa, check the specific eligibility criteria for that visa type. Each visa category has different requirements, such as:

- Valid passport.
- Proof of funds to cover your stay.
- English language proficiency (for work and study visas).
- Sponsorship (for work visas).
- Acceptance from a UK educational institution (for student visas).

Carefully review the eligibility requirements for the visa type you are applying for to ensure you meet all the conditions before proceeding.

Step 3: Complete the Online Visa Application Form

The next step is to complete the visa application form online through the official UK government website. The application form will ask for essential details, including:

- Personal information (name, date of birth, passport details).
- Travel plans (arrival and departure dates, flight details, accommodation).
- Reason for visiting the UK (tourism, work, study, etc.).
- Financial information (proof of funds, bank statements, etc.).

Make sure to double-check your answers and provide accurate information, as discrepancies can delay or even result in the rejection of your application.

Step 4: Pay the Visa Application Fee

Once you've completed the online application form, you will be required to pay the visa application fee. The cost of the visa varies depending on the type of visa and its duration. For example:

- **Standard Visitor Visa:** Around £95 (for up to 6 months).
- **Skilled Worker Visa:** £610–£1,408, depending on the job and length of stay.
- **Student Visa:** Around £348 for most applicants.

You can pay the visa fee online using a credit or debit card. Be sure to keep a copy of your payment receipt, as you'll need it for your records.

Step 5: Gather Required Documents

To support your visa application, you'll need to gather several essential documents, which may include:

- **Passport:** A valid passport with at least one page available for the visa stamp.
- **Passport-sized photograph:** A recent passport-style photo as per UK visa photo requirements.
- **Proof of funds:** Bank statements, pay slips, or evidence of financial support to prove you can afford your stay.
- **Travel itinerary:** Details of your flights, accommodation, and planned activities during your trip.
- **Sponsorship or offer letter:** For work or study visas, provide your certificate of sponsorship or acceptance letter from a UK employer or educational institution.
- **English language proficiency:** If required, provide proof of your English language skills (via an approved test like IELTS).
- **Tuberculosis test:** If applicable, especially for applicants from certain countries.

Ensure that you have all the required documents in their proper format and that they meet the specifications outlined on the UK government website.

Step 6: Book Your Biometric Appointment

After submitting your visa application form and paying the fee, you will be required to book a biometric appointment at a visa application center (VAC) in your home country. During this appointment, you will:

- Have your fingerprints taken.
- Have your photograph taken.

The biometric appointment is a crucial part of the visa application process, and it is typically required for all visa applicants (except for certain countries or visa categories).

Step 7: Submit Your Application and Attend Your Appointment

Once you've completed all the steps, submit your visa application, along with your documents, either online or at a designated visa application center (depending on the visa type). For biometric appointments, ensure that you bring all the necessary documents, including:

- Your passport.
- Payment receipt.
- Biometric appointment confirmation.
- Any other documents requested by the VAC.

Some visa types may require additional documentation or an interview, so be prepared for further steps.

Step 8: Wait for a Decision

After attending your biometric appointment and submitting your application, you will need to wait for a decision. The processing time varies based on the visa type and location. As a general guideline:

- **Standard Visitor Visa:** Around 3 weeks.
- **Skilled Worker Visa:** Around 8 weeks.
- **Student Visa:** Around 8 weeks.

You can track the status of your visa application online through the UK government's application tracking system.

Step 9: Receive Your Visa Decision

Once your visa application has been processed, you will receive a decision. If your visa is approved, you will be issued a visa vignette (sticker) in your passport, which will allow you to enter the UK. If your application is refused, you will receive a letter outlining the reasons for the refusal and your options for appeal or reapplication.

Step 10: Travel to the UK

If your visa application is successful, you can make your travel arrangements to Bristol. Ensure that you carry all the necessary documents with you during your travel, including your passport, visa, and any additional supporting documentation.

The UK visa application process may seem complex at first, but by following these steps, you can ensure that you meet all the requirements and submit a thorough application. It's essential to apply well in advance of your planned travel dates, as processing times can vary. Additionally, ensure that you are aware of any updates to visa regulations or entry requirements, especially in light of ongoing changes in travel policies.

By following this step-by-step guide, you'll be one step closer to enjoying your time in Bristol, whether you're visiting for business, study, or leisure.

When and Where to Apply for Visas

Applying for a UK visa requires careful planning, especially when considering the right timing and location to submit your application. Understanding when and where to apply can help streamline your travel plans, ensuring that you meet all the entry requirements without unnecessary delays. Below is a detailed overview of when and where to apply for UK visas, based on the purpose of your visit.

When to Apply for a UK Visa

The timing of your visa application is crucial to avoid unnecessary stress or delays before your planned travel to Bristol. Here are some key points to consider regarding when to apply:

1. Application Timing for Different Visa Types

- **Standard Visitor Visa:** For tourism, business, or family visits, it's recommended to apply for your visa at least **3 months** before your planned travel date. Processing times for a standard visitor visa are typically around **3 weeks**.

- **Work Visa:** For skilled workers or anyone applying for a visa tied to employment in the UK, the application process can take longer. It's advisable to submit your application at least **8 weeks** before your job start date. Processing times can vary, but it typically takes **8 weeks** for skilled worker visa applications.

- **Student Visa:** If you plan to study in the UK, you should apply for your student visa at least **3 months** in advance of your course start date. The processing time for student visas is usually around **8 weeks**.

- **Transit Visa:** If you're passing through the UK en route to another destination, applying at least **3 weeks** before your departure is generally recommended. The processing time is usually around **15 working days**.

2. How Early Can You Apply?

- You can submit your visa application **up to 3 months** in advance of your intended date of arrival in the UK (or up to **6 months** for certain visas such as the long-term visitor visa). However, it's important to apply well in advance, especially if there are any complications or additional requirements, such as the need for biometric information or medical checks.

3. What Happens If You Apply Too Late?

- While it is possible to apply for a visa on short notice, it is highly discouraged to leave it to the last minute. UK visa processing times can fluctuate, and submitting a late application may result in missed travel plans. It's best to aim for a minimum of **8 weeks** ahead of your trip, especially if applying for work or study visas that require additional processing.

Where to Apply for a UK Visa

Visa applications for the UK must be submitted at specific locations, either online or in person at visa application centers (VACs). Here's where and how to apply for a UK visa:

1. Online Applications

For most UK visa categories, the application process begins online through the official UK government website. Here's how to proceed:

- **Online Visa Application Portal:** You can complete your visa application form and pay the application fee online through the official **UK Visa and Immigration (UKVI)** website. The website provides all the necessary forms for various types of visas, along with instructions for filling out your application correctly.

- **Documents Submission:** After submitting the online form, you will be directed to a visa application center to provide supporting documents and biometric data. However, note that some specific visas, like the Electronic Visa Waiver (EVW), can be completed entirely online, depending on your nationality.

- **Tracking Your Application:** Once your visa application is submitted online, you can track its progress via the application portal.

2. Visa Application Centers (VACs)

After completing your online visa application, you will likely need to attend a **Visa Application Center (VAC)** to submit your biometric details (fingerprints and photograph). These centers are typically located in major cities worldwide, including locations such as:

- **Bristol's Nearest VAC:** If you're applying from outside the UK, locate your nearest VAC using the UK government's online tools. In some cases, VACs are located in neighboring cities or larger metropolitan areas. For example, applicants from nearby countries or cities may need to travel to London or other regional centers to complete the biometric process.

- **Appointment Scheduling:** Once you complete your online application, you'll need to schedule an appointment at a local VAC to submit your documents and provide biometric data. It's essential to make your appointment well in advance, as VACs can sometimes have limited availability.

- **Document Submission:** Depending on the visa type, you may need to bring documents like your passport, proof of finances, a letter of invitation, or proof of accommodation to your VAC appointment.

3. Application via the Post (for Specific Cases)

In some cases, the UK visa application process can also be done via post, particularly if you're applying from within the UK for a different visa or for an extension. This will require you to send all your documents to the appropriate UKVI office, along with the visa fee payment. However, this option is usually less common for initial visa applications.

Regional Considerations for Where to Apply

While VACs are available in many countries, the process of applying for a visa might slightly differ based on your location. Some countries or regions may have additional requirements, such as the need for a tuberculosis (TB) test or additional documentation related to travel history or previous visas. Ensure you check the official UK visa website for specific requirements for your country of residence.

Additional Required Documents for UK Visa Applications

When applying for a UK visa, the standard documents required will typically include your passport, application form, and biometric data. However, there are various additional documents that you might need to submit depending on the type of visa you're applying for. Below is a detailed list of potential additional documents you may be required to provide:

1. Proof of Identity

- **Passport**: A valid passport that must be valid for at least 6 months beyond your intended stay in the UK.
- **Photographs**: Recent passport-sized color photos that meet UKVI specifications. These are typically required during your biometric appointment.

2. Proof of Financial Means

- **Bank Statements**: Recent bank statements (typically the last 3 months) showing sufficient funds to support your stay in the UK.
- **Pay Slips**: If employed, you may need to submit your latest pay slips (usually for the last 3 to 6 months).
- **Sponsorship Letter**: If someone in the UK is sponsoring you, you will need a letter from them confirming their financial support, along with their bank statements and proof of identity.

3. Proof of Accommodation

- **Accommodation Booking**: If staying in a hotel, provide a booking confirmation. If staying with friends or family, you may need to submit an invitation letter from your host along with proof of their residence.
- **Rental Agreement**: For longer stays, a rental agreement may be requested as proof of where you will be staying.

4. Travel Itinerary

- **Flight Tickets**: Some visa types, especially tourist visas, may require you to show your planned travel dates, including inbound and outbound flight tickets.
- **Travel Insurance**: While not always required, travel insurance that covers medical expenses, cancellation, and travel delays is highly recommended and may be requested for longer stays or specific types of visas.

5. Purpose of Visit Documents

Depending on the type of visa, you may need to provide supporting documents that outline the purpose of your trip:

- **Tourist Visa**: A detailed travel itinerary including the places you plan to visit, accommodation details, and any planned

activities or tours.
- **Work Visa**: An offer of employment or a sponsorship letter from your employer in the UK.
- **Student Visa**: A confirmation of enrollment (e.g., a CAS letter) from a UK educational institution.
- **Business Visa**: If traveling for business, provide a letter of invitation from the company or organization you are visiting, along with any business contracts or event invitations.

6. Proof of Relationship (For Family Visas)

- **Marriage Certificate**: If you are applying for a family visa (e.g., to join a spouse or partner), you may need to submit your marriage certificate or other proof of the relationship, such as photographs, communication logs, or other evidence.
- **Children's Birth Certificates**: If traveling with children, their birth certificates or adoption papers may be requested.

7. English Language Proficiency (For Certain Visa Types)

- **English Language Test Results**: If required, proof of your ability to speak and understand English is essential. For many visa types, you will need to provide results from a recognized English language test, such as IELTS.
- **Academic Qualifications**: If you're applying for a student visa, you may need to show proof of prior qualifications or your academic history.

8. Tuberculosis (TB) Test Results

- **TB Test**: If you are applying for a visa from certain countries (mostly from outside the European Economic Area), you may be required to undergo a tuberculosis (TB) test. A certificate from an approved clinic will be necessary to submit with your application.

9. Police Clearance Certificate (For Certain Visas)

- **Police Certificate**: For some long-term visas, such as those for work or study, you may be required to submit a police clearance certificate from your home country or any country where you have lived for more than 12 months over the past 10 years.

10. Health and Character Requirements (For Long-Term Visas)

- **Health Declaration**: Some visa applicants, especially those applying for long-term stays, may be asked to submit a medical report or declaration confirming they do not have any serious health conditions.
- **Character Reference**: For certain visa types, such as work visas or family reunification, you may be asked to submit a character reference or evidence that you have no serious criminal record.

11. Additional Documents for Specific Visa Types

- **Visitor Visa**: For visitors intending to travel to the UK for a short stay (tourism, family visits, business), you may need to provide additional documents such as:
    - A letter from your employer or a leave letter confirming your employment status and return to your home country.
    - Evidence of your ties to your home country, such as property ownership, family dependents, or other commitments that demonstrate your intention to return home.
- **Entrepreneur or Investor Visa**: If applying for an entrepreneur or investor visa, additional documentation will include proof of the required funds, a detailed business plan, and evidence of the source of your investment funds.

How to Submit Documents

- **Original Documents and Copies**: You must bring original documents to the Visa Application Center (VAC) or submit them through the online portal if specified. You will also be required to provide photocopies of all supporting documents.
- **Translations**: Any documents not in English will need to be translated into English by a certified translator. This includes birth certificates, marriage certificates, academic transcripts, and other official documents.

The required additional documents for your UK visa application can vary depending on the type of visa you are applying for and your personal circumstances. Be sure to review the official UK visa guidelines specific to your visa category to ensure that you gather all necessary paperwork. Submitting the right documents in a timely manner will help ensure that your visa application is processed efficiently, allowing you to enjoy your trip to Bristol without any setbacks.

LOCAL CUSTOMS AND ETIQUETTE

Cultural Norms and Practices in Bristol

Bristol is a city steeped in history, and its residents take pride in their rich cultural traditions. The city's culture is a vibrant mix of contemporary urban living and a deep appreciation for its historical past. Understanding the local cultural norms and practices can greatly enhance your experience when visiting. Here are some key aspects of Bristol's cultural norms and practices that every traveler should know:

1. Respect for Diversity

Bristol is known for its diverse population, and this is reflected in the city's cultural practices. People from all walks of life live and work together harmoniously, contributing to the city's cosmopolitan atmosphere. The city embraces multiculturalism, and you'll find a variety of festivals, events, and eateries that showcase the diversity of its residents. Whether you're enjoying the local music scene, tasting cuisine from around the world, or attending cultural events, it's essential to embrace and respect this diversity.

- **Local Tip**: Be open to experiencing different cultures, cuisines, and traditions that you might encounter while in Bristol. Showing curiosity and respect for others' cultures will be appreciated.

2. Politeness and Courtesy

Like much of the UK, Bristolian culture places a high value on politeness and courtesy. Greetings are important, and it's customary to greet people with a handshake or a friendly smile. Saying "please" and "thank you" is not only expected but appreciated in all interactions, whether in stores, restaurants, or in conversations with locals. Being polite and respectful goes a long way in establishing positive relationships.

- **Local Tip**: When asking for directions or assistance, use "Excuse me" as a polite introduction to your request. A simple "thank you" after receiving help will always be well received.

3. Queuing (Standing in Line)

Queueing, or waiting your turn in line, is a deeply ingrained practice in Bristol, as it is across the UK. Whether you're at the bus stop, in a grocery store, or waiting to get into a popular restaurant, make sure to stand in line and wait your turn. Jumping ahead of someone in line is considered rude, and locals may react negatively if this happens.

- **Local Tip**: When entering shops or public transportation, wait for others to exit before you enter. Always respect the line and be mindful of personal space.

4. Punctuality

Punctuality is important in Bristol, as it is throughout the UK. Arriving late, especially for work or scheduled appointments, is generally seen as disrespectful. Whether you're attending a meeting, catching a train, or heading to a reservation at a restaurant, make sure to be on time.

- **Local Tip**: Aim to arrive at least 10-15 minutes early for appointments or events to avoid being seen as late. If you are running late, always call ahead to inform the concerned party.

5. Tipping Etiquette

In Bristol, tipping is not mandatory but is appreciated for good service. In restaurants, it is common to leave a tip of 10-15% of the bill if service is not included in the price. If service is included, a tip is not necessary, but you are still welcome to leave a small amount if you feel the service was exceptional. Tipping taxi drivers and hotel staff is also customary, though the amount is at your discretion.

- **Local Tip**: Always check if a service charge is already included in your restaurant bill before tipping. For small services like taxi rides or bellhops, rounding up the fare is typical.

6. Dress Code

While Bristol is a relaxed and casual city, there are certain occasions when dressing up is appropriate. In more formal settings like fine dining restaurants, theaters, or certain upscale events, smart casual or formal attire is expected. However, on a typical day out exploring the city or visiting casual cafes and bars, locals tend to dress comfortably and casually.

- **Local Tip**: For visits to formal events, it's better to be slightly overdressed than underdressed. If you're unsure, it's always a safe bet to ask about the dress code beforehand.

7. Environmental Consciousness

Bristol is known for its commitment to sustainability and environmental consciousness. The city takes pride in its green initiatives, from bike-sharing schemes to recycling programs. Locals are typically very mindful of waste reduction and eco-friendly practices. It's common to see people bringing reusable shopping bags, recycling their waste, and using public transportation or bicycles instead of driving.

- **Local Tip**: Make an effort to recycle, avoid littering, and consider using public transportation or walking to explore the city in an environmentally conscious manner. Many restaurants and stores also encourage using reusable containers.

8. Taboos and Sensitivities

While Bristol is an open-minded and progressive city, there are a few sensitive topics that you should be mindful of. Discussions around race, class, and politics can sometimes lead to heated debates, so it's best to approach these subjects with care and respect. Always be open-minded and avoid making assumptions or generalizations about individuals or groups.

- **Local Tip**: If you're unsure about discussing sensitive topics, steer the conversation toward neutral subjects like food, travel, or local events. This way, you can avoid any discomfort while still enjoying meaningful interactions.

9. Public Behavior and Social Etiquette

Bristol has a generally laid-back attitude toward public behavior, but it's important to be aware of how your actions might affect others. Public displays of affection are not uncommon but should be kept respectful and considerate of those around you. Loud or disruptive behavior, especially in public spaces like public transport or cafes, is frowned upon.

- **Local Tip**: Keep noise levels low in public spaces, be mindful of your surroundings, and avoid disruptive behavior that could inconvenience others.

10. Festivals and Celebrations

Bristol is known for its lively cultural festivals and celebrations, which include events like the Bristol International Balloon Fiesta, St. Paul's Carnival, and Bristol Harbour Festival. These festivals celebrate the city's multiculturalism, music, arts, and history. Participating in local festivals is a wonderful way to experience the culture and meet friendly locals.

- **Local Tip**: If you're in Bristol during one of its major festivals, be sure to join in the celebrations. Locals are welcoming, and you'll get a chance to experience the city's community spirit at its best.

Understanding the cultural norms and practices in Bristol can significantly enhance your travel experience. Whether it's respecting personal space, engaging with the local community, or embracing the city's diverse culture, being mindful of these cultural guidelines will help you navigate the city with ease and confidence. In return, you'll gain a deeper appreciation for Bristol's unique blend of tradition, modernity, and inclusivity.

Dos and Don'ts for Visitors in Bristol

Bristol is a vibrant and welcoming city, offering a rich cultural experience for all who visit. However, as with any place, there are certain customs and social norms that visitors should be mindful of to ensure they have a smooth and enjoyable stay. Here's a guide to the dos and don'ts that will help you navigate Bristol's social landscape with ease and respect.

Dos:

1. Do Greet People Politely

Bristol, like the rest of the UK, values politeness and good manners. It's customary to greet people with a smile and a simple "hello" or "good morning" when entering shops, cafes, or other public spaces. When meeting someone for the first time, a handshake is a common gesture of greeting, though it is not as formal as in some cultures.

- **Local Tip:** When asking for directions or assistance, always start with "Excuse me" to show respect and politeness.

2. Do Embrace the City's Diversity

Bristol is a melting pot of cultures and communities, and embracing this diversity is key to understanding the city. Whether it's enjoying international cuisine, attending multicultural festivals, or engaging in conversation with locals from all walks of life, show interest in the cultural differences you encounter.

- **Local Tip:** Participate in local events or festivals to experience the city's multicultural flair, such as the St. Paul's Carnival or the Bristol International Balloon Fiesta.

3. Do Respect the Environment

Bristol is committed to sustainability and environmental preservation. Recycling, reducing waste, and using eco-friendly options like public transport or bicycles are highly valued by the locals. It's important to adopt these practices during your visit.

- **Local Tip:** Be mindful of littering—always dispose of your waste properly, and consider using the city's bike-share scheme for eco-friendly travel.

4. Do Mind Your Queueing

Queueing (standing in line) is a highly respected practice in the UK, and Bristol is no exception. Whether you're waiting for a bus, at a bus stop, in a supermarket, or at a popular cafe, always stand in line and wait your turn. Skipping ahead in the queue is considered impolite.

- **Local Tip:** If in doubt, follow the lead of others and wait in line quietly until it's your turn.

5. Do Be Punctual

Punctuality is a sign of respect in Bristol, particularly in professional or formal settings. Arriving late is often seen as inconsiderate, especially for scheduled events, meetings, or dinner reservations.

- **Local Tip:** Aim to arrive 10-15 minutes early for appointments or reservations, especially when traveling for business or dining in higher-end restaurants.

6. Do Tip for Good Service

While tipping isn't mandatory in the UK, it is appreciated for good service. In restaurants, it's typical to leave a tip of 10-15% of the bill if service is not included. For taxi rides, rounding up the fare is a kind gesture, and hotel staff may appreciate small tips for carrying luggage or assisting with services.

- **Local Tip:** Check your restaurant bill to see if a service charge has been added before leaving a tip. If not, aim to leave around 10-15% for excellent service.

Don'ts:

1. Don't Be Too Loud

British culture tends to favor reserved and quiet behavior in public spaces. Bristol is no exception, and while it is a lively city with plenty of entertainment options, being excessively loud, especially in quieter areas like public transport or cafes, can be seen as disruptive.

- **Local Tip:** Keep your conversations at a moderate volume in public spaces, and be considerate of others around you.

2. Don't Jump Ahead in the Queue

Queueing is sacred in Bristol, and jumping ahead of others is one of the biggest social faux pas. Whether you're waiting for a bus, in a store, or at a restaurant, make sure to wait your turn.

- **Local Tip:** If you're unsure where the queue starts, wait for a local to guide you or follow the line to ensure you're standing in the right spot.

3. Don't Discuss Sensitive Topics Unnecessarily

While locals are friendly and open-minded, it's wise to avoid discussing sensitive topics like politics, religion, or personal finances, unless you know the person well and feel the conversation is appropriate. These subjects can often lead to discomfort or disagreement if approached too casually.

- **Local Tip:** Stick to light-hearted topics such as the weather, local attractions, or events to avoid inadvertently crossing any boundaries.

4. Don't Assume Everyone Is From Bristol

While Bristol is a city with a strong local identity, it's a hub for people from various regions of the UK and abroad. Don't assume that everyone you meet is a local Bristolian. Many visitors and people from other parts of the UK live in Bristol, so it's best not to make assumptions based on accents or appearances.

- **Local Tip:** If you're unsure, you can always ask where someone is from. It can be a great conversation starter!

5. Don't Forget to Respect Personal Space

In Bristol, as in much of the UK, respecting personal space is important. Locals tend to maintain a certain amount of physical distance, especially in more formal settings or crowded spaces like public transport. Avoid standing too close to others, and be mindful of people's personal space.

- **Local Tip:** If you're in a crowded area or public transport, try to keep your distance from others, especially if they seem to be in their own personal space bubble.

6. Don't Engage in Public Displays of Affection (PDA) Excessively

While some public displays of affection, such as holding hands or a quick kiss, are generally acceptable, excessive PDA can be seen as inappropriate in certain public spaces, particularly in more reserved areas or in front of strangers.

- **Local Tip:** It's best to keep public displays of affection subtle and respectful to the local customs, especially when in formal or public settings.

Understanding the dos and don'ts of Bristol's local customs and etiquette will help you make the most of your visit while ensuring you interact respectfully with the locals. By following these simple guidelines, you'll blend in seamlessly with the city's residents, showing your appreciation for their cultural norms and traditions, and making your experience all the more enjoyable and enriching. Whether it's embracing the city's diversity, respecting personal space, or simply minding your manners, being considerate of these customs will leave a positive impression and help you truly immerse yourself in the Bristolian way of life.

How to Blend in Like a Local in Bristol

Bristol is a dynamic, diverse city where locals take pride in their unique cultural identity. For visitors hoping to blend in like a local, it's important to understand the social norms, attitudes, and behaviors that are common in the city. While Bristol is open and welcoming, being mindful of its customs will help you embrace the city's laid-back yet respectful atmosphere and make the most of your time there.

Here's a guide to blending in like a true Bristolian:

1. Adopt the Local Pace of Life

Bristol is known for its relaxed and laid-back vibe, but that doesn't mean it's a sleepy town. Locals appreciate a balanced lifestyle, so while they are busy during the workweek, they also know how to enjoy their leisure time. Avoid rushing through the streets or forcing yourself to keep up with a hectic pace. Instead, embrace the slower tempo, take your time to enjoy the sights, and participate in leisurely activities like grabbing a coffee at a local café or walking along the harborside.

- **Local Tip:** If you're walking through the city, take time to enjoy the surroundings, whether it's the historic architecture or the stunning street art. Bristol is a city that rewards curiosity.

2. Respect the City's Local Pride

Bristol is a city that has a strong sense of local pride. From its rich maritime history to its thriving music scene, Bristolians are proud of their roots. As a visitor, expressing an appreciation for the city's history and culture will earn you respect. Take the time to learn about the city's background, whether it's the importance of the port, the legacy of the Bristol Channel, or its modern-day cultural significance. Show respect for local initiatives, such as sustainable living and community-driven events.

- **Local Tip:** Attend local festivals or events like the Bristol International Balloon Fiesta or the Bristol Harbour Festival to engage with the city's culture and make connections with locals.

3. Embrace the Bristolian Sense of Humor

Bristolians have a distinctive sense of humor, often characterized by wit and sarcasm. They enjoy banter, but it's important to gauge the situation before diving into humor, especially if you're unfamiliar with the area. Don't take things too seriously, and try to adopt a playful and easygoing attitude when interacting with locals. Show that you can enjoy a good laugh, especially with the regional dialect and colloquial expressions that often come with it.

- **Local Tip:** If someone cracks a joke or uses local slang, laugh along! It's a sign that you're embracing the local culture, even if you don't fully understand everything being said.

4. Use the Local Lingo (But Don't Overdo It)

Bristol has its own dialect and way of speaking, which is heavily influenced by its history and working-class roots. While you don't need to speak like a local, picking up a few key phrases can help you connect with residents and show that you're trying to integrate. For example, "luv" is a common friendly term used in conversation, and "gert lush" is used to describe something great or amazing. However, be mindful not to overdo it, as locals can spot someone trying too hard.

- **Local Tip:** When in doubt, keep it simple and polite. A friendly "Alright?" (pronounced as "Ah-right?") is a casual greeting in Bristol that's both approachable and widely used.

5. Be Mindful of Local Sustainability Efforts

Bristol is a city known for its strong commitment to sustainability and environmental responsibility. Locals are dedicated to reducing waste, supporting green initiatives, and maintaining the city's clean and natural surroundings. To blend in, consider using public transportation, cycling, or walking instead of driving. Take part in recycling efforts and avoid littering. You'll fit in well with the local crowd if you adopt eco-friendly practices.

- **Local Tip:** Many cafes and restaurants in Bristol encourage customers to bring their own reusable cups or containers. Don't forget to do your part by embracing these sustainable practices.

6. Get Involved in the Coffee Culture

Bristol has a fantastic coffee culture, and whether you're stopping for a morning brew or meeting friends for a casual catch-up, coffee shops are central to daily life. Locals often opt for specialty coffee, and Bristol is home to numerous independent cafes offering high-quality, locally roasted coffee. Don't just grab a quick takeaway; sit down and enjoy the experience. It's common to spend time at a local café, either alone or with friends, as part of the daily routine.

- **Local Tip:** Try "Bristol Blend" coffee or order something unique, like a flat white, which is a popular choice in the city. You'll easily blend in with the locals by enjoying coffee in a relaxed manner.

7. Dress with a Casual Yet Stylish Edge

Bristol is known for its eclectic style, with a mix of bohemian, vintage, and modern influences. Locals have a laid-back yet fashionable sense of dressing, often mixing high-street fashion with quirky, individual pieces. You won't find people overly dressed up in Bristol, but there's an appreciation for personal style and comfort. It's a good idea to pack comfortable yet stylish clothes that can be worn for both day and night activities, from exploring the harborside to visiting trendy neighborhoods like Clifton or Stokes Croft.

- **Local Tip:** If you're heading to a more formal event, don't go overboard with a suit or dress—opt for something smart-casual to blend in seamlessly with the locals.

8. Show Respect for Local Pubs and Live Music Venues

The pub is at the heart of Bristol's social life. Local pubs and music venues are important cultural hubs where Bristolians socialize, relax, and enjoy live music performances. Whether you're popping into a traditional pub for a pint of cider or attending a gig at a smaller venue, be respectful of the local pub culture. Always buy a drink when you enter a pub and don't overstay your welcome after closing time. At live music venues, it's common to show your appreciation for the performers by clapping and cheering.

- **Local Tip:** Check out local favorite pubs like The Coronation Tap or Thekla for a true Bristolian experience, and always keep an eye out for local bands playing live.

9. Be Open to Exploring the Hidden Gems

Bristol is a city full of hidden gems, and to blend in with the locals, make sure to explore its lesser-known spots. While tourist attractions like the Clifton Suspension Bridge and Bristol Zoo are iconic, Bristolians also appreciate the city's lesser-explored areas. Visit the vibrant street art scene in Stokes Croft, check out the independent shops in Gloucester Road, or wander around the creative spaces at the Arnolfini Arts Centre. Locals love sharing tips about the city's off-the-beaten-path experiences.

- **Local Tip:** Ask a local for their favorite secret spot in the city—you'll likely get an insider's recommendation that will make your trip even more memorable.

Blending in like a local in Bristol requires an openness to the city's relaxed vibe, appreciation for its diverse culture, and respect for its unique customs. By adopting the local pace, engaging with the community, and following these simple tips, you'll be well on your way to embracing the Bristolian way of life. Whether you're enjoying a coffee in a cozy café, participating in a lively conversation, or exploring the city's sustainable initiatives, being mindful of local norms will help you connect with the people and the place in a more meaningful way.

INSIGHT TIPS

Budget-Saving Hacks for Travelers in Bristol

Traveling to Bristol on a budget doesn't mean sacrificing quality experiences or missing out on the city's vibrant atmosphere. With a bit of insider knowledge, you can enjoy the best of Bristol while keeping your expenses in check. From free activities to affordable eating options, here are some top budget-saving hacks to make the most of your trip without breaking the bank.

1. Take Advantage of Free Attractions and Museums

Bristol is a city with a rich history and a thriving cultural scene, and there are plenty of attractions that won't cost you a penny. Many of the city's museums and galleries offer free admission, making them perfect for budget-conscious travelers.

- **The Bristol Museum & Art Gallery**: Explore the diverse collections from art to natural history. It's free to enter, and you can easily spend hours admiring the exhibits.
- **M Shed**: This local history museum on the harbor tells the story of Bristol's past and is entirely free to enter.
- **Street Art Tour**: Bristol is known for its vibrant street art

scene, and the best part is, it's all free! Take a walk around areas like Stokes Croft and the Old City to discover works by famous artists like Banksy.

2. Visit the Parks and Outdoor Spaces

Bristol boasts an array of beautiful green spaces, perfect for a day of relaxation, picnics, or outdoor exploration—all free of charge. These parks are ideal for those who want to enjoy the city's natural beauty without spending any money.

- **Brandon Hill and Cabot Tower**: Climb up Cabot Tower for panoramic views of the city, or simply wander around Brandon Hill, a beautiful park with tranquil walking paths.
- **Ashton Court Estate**: A vast parkland offering woodlands, rolling hills, and outdoor activities such as cycling and hiking. It's a fantastic place for a day out without any costs.
- **Queen Square**: A picturesque green space in the heart of the city that's perfect for relaxing and people-watching, especially during the warmer months.

3. Take Public Transport or Walk

Bristol's public transport system is quite affordable, and for many attractions, walking is a great way to explore the city. Rather than splurging on taxis or rideshares, consider using buses or even cycling around.

- **Buy a Day Saver Ticket**: For unlimited travel on buses throughout the city, purchase a day saver ticket, which gives you access to multiple journeys for a set price. This is especially useful if you plan on visiting several areas in one day.
- **Walking Tours**: If you're interested in learning more about the city, free walking tours are a great option. Many tour companies offer "pay-what-you-think-it's-worth" walking tours, where you pay the guide a tip based on your experience.

4. Opt for Affordable, High-Quality Food

Bristol is known for its thriving food scene, but you don't have to break the bank to enjoy delicious meals. There are plenty of budget-friendly food options that still let you experience the city's culinary offerings.

- **Street Food**: Head to the Wapping Wharf or St. Nicholas Market to find a wide range of street food vendors offering meals for under £10. From Asian street food to gourmet burgers, you can find tasty and filling meals without spending much.
- **Vegan and Vegetarian Options**: Bristol is renowned for its vegan and vegetarian food scene. Many eateries offer affordable plant-based options that are both delicious and budget-friendly. Try places like **The Eden Project** or **Veggie World** at St. Nicholas Market for healthy, inexpensive meals.
- **Lunch Specials**: Many restaurants in Bristol offer lunch deals or set menus that are far cheaper than dinner options. Look out for these deals in cafes, pubs, and casual dining restaurants for a more affordable meal.

5. Use Discount Cards and Deals

Before your trip, take advantage of discount cards and online deals to save money on attractions and activities.

- **Bristol Visitor Card**: This card gives you discounts to major attractions, galleries, and museums, as well as special offers in restaurants and shops. It's a great way to save while experiencing the city's top spots.
- **Groupon and Other Discount Sites**: Check sites like Groupon for discounted tickets and deals on tours, activities, and restaurant vouchers. You can often find substantial discounts for local attractions or even for things like afternoon teas and guided city tours.

6. Take Advantage of Happy Hours and Early Bird Specials

If you enjoy dining out but want to keep costs down, be sure to take advantage of happy hour deals or early bird specials at Bristol's pubs and restaurants.

- **Happy Hour**: Many bars and pubs in the city offer happy hour specials, where drinks and sometimes small plates are offered at reduced prices. Look out for deals at local spots such as **The Bristol Yard** or **The Canteen** in Stokes Croft.
- **Early Bird Menus**: If you're looking for a sit-down meal without the high price tag, several restaurants in Bristol offer early bird specials or pre-theatre menus, which allow you to enjoy a full meal at a more affordable price.

7. Stay in Budget-Friendly Accommodation

Accommodation is often one of the biggest expenses for travelers. Luckily, Bristol offers a variety of affordable lodging options, so you don't have to break the bank when booking your stay.

- **Hostels and Budget Hotels**: Bristol is home to several well-rated hostels, such as **Rock n Bowl Hostel** and **Bristol Backpackers Hostel**, which provide basic, comfortable accommodation at a fraction of the price of hotels.
- **Airbnb**: Renting a room or apartment through Airbnb can be a budget-friendly way to stay in the city, especially if you're traveling with a group. Look for listings near transport links or within walking distance of key attractions.
- **University Halls**: During the summer months, university halls of residence open up to travelers as a budget-friendly accommodation option. These can be a great alternative to pricier hotels, and they're often centrally located.

8. Be Strategic About Souvenirs

When shopping for souvenirs, it's easy to overspend on items that won't hold much value. Be mindful of where you buy your mementos and look for local markets and independent shops that offer unique, reasonably priced items.

- **St. Nicholas Market**: This indoor market is a goldmine for affordable, locally crafted goods. From handmade jewelry to vintage clothing, you'll find plenty of unique souvenirs at budget-friendly prices.
- **Vintage Shops**: Bristol is full of great vintage and charity shops, where you can score second-hand treasures like clothing, records, and artwork without paying full price.

9. Plan Your Activities Ahead of Time

One of the best ways to save money while traveling in Bristol is to plan ahead. Look up free activities, research discounts, and check opening hours to make sure you're getting the best value for your money.

- **Research City Events**: Many festivals, concerts, and events in Bristol are free or low-cost. Plan your trip around these activities to experience the best of the city without spending a lot.
- **Plan Your Routes Efficiently**: Instead of spending money on multiple modes of transport, plan your routes to take in multiple attractions or neighborhoods in one go. This not only saves on transport costs but also allows you to explore more of the city.

Bristol offers a wealth of experiences that cater to all types of travelers, even those on a budget. By taking advantage of free attractions, exploring local food markets, and using money-saving tips like public transport, affordable dining options, and discount cards, you can experience the best of the city without overspending. Whether you're visiting for a weekend or a longer stay, these budget-saving hacks will help you enjoy all that Bristol has to offer while keeping your finances in check.

Hidden Gems Only Locals Know in Bristol

Bristol is a city brimming with character, and while its most famous attractions are certainly worth a visit, the true charm of the city often lies in its lesser-known spots. From tucked-away cafés to secret gardens, here are some hidden gems in Bristol that only the locals truly know about. Whether you're looking for a peaceful escape, unique shopping experiences, or a taste of Bristol's eclectic vibe, these spots will give you an insider's view of the city.

1. The Bristol Lido

- **Location**: Oakfield Place, Clifton, Bristol BS8 2BJ
- **Overview**: One of Bristol's best-kept secrets, the Lido is a hidden gem tucked away in the charming Clifton neighborhood. This stunning, restored Victorian outdoor swimming pool offers a unique blend of history, beauty, and relaxation. The heated pool is surrounded by lush greenery, providing a peaceful oasis in the heart of the city. Alongside the pool, there's a beautiful spa, a café, and a restaurant, making it the perfect place for a rejuvenating afternoon.
- **Why It's a Hidden Gem**: Many visitors overlook the Lido in favor of more well-known attractions, but locals know this spot as an idyllic escape from the bustle of the city. Whether you're taking a swim or simply relaxing in the spa, it's an experience that feels miles away from the urban hustle.

2. Redcliffe Caves

- **Location**: Redcliffe, Bristol BS1 6PR
- **Overview**: Beneath the bustling streets of Redcliffe lies a series of historic caves that are largely unknown to the public. These caves, dating back to the 16th century, were once used for various purposes, including storage and even

as a secretive hideaway. Today, they offer a fascinating glimpse into the city's hidden past. The caves are occasionally open to the public through guided tours, revealing a part of Bristol's history that most visitors never get to see.
- **Why It's a Hidden Gem**: Access to these caves is limited, and their obscure location makes them one of Bristol's best-hidden secrets. Few tourists venture here, but those who do are treated to an atmospheric journey back in time.

3. The Christmas Steps

- **Location**: Christmas Steps, City Centre, Bristol BS1 5BS
- **Overview**: Tucked away in the heart of the city, the Christmas Steps are an ancient, narrow set of stairs that lead up to a quaint cobbled street filled with independent shops, galleries, and cafés. The area, rich in history, dates back to the medieval period and has retained much of its charm over the centuries. It's one of the most photogenic spots in Bristol, with its beautifully preserved architecture and unique character.
- **Why It's a Hidden Gem**: Although the Christmas Steps are located in a central area, they often go unnoticed by visitors who stick to the main tourist routes. The area around the steps is a peaceful retreat from the city's busier streets, offering an authentic, off-the-beaten-path experience.

4. The Floating Harbour

- **Location**: Bristol Harbour, City Centre
- **Overview**: Bristol's Floating Harbour is a historic waterway that was once at the heart of the city's maritime trade. Today, it's a tranquil spot perfect for a leisurely stroll, but what many visitors don't know is that the harbour has plenty of hidden spots that locals cherish. From hidden café terraces on barges to quiet docks where you can watch the boats go by, there are many serene pockets to explore. For an even more unique experience, take a boat trip to get an up-close view of

the city's maritime history.
- **Why It's a Hidden Gem**: The Floating Harbour is well-known, but locals tend to frequent the less commercialized parts of it, away from the large tourist attractions. If you seek a peaceful, scenic area away from the crowds, this is the place to be.

5. St. Nicholas Market

- **Location**: Corn Street, Bristol BS1 1JQ
- **Overview**: While St. Nicholas Market is a popular spot for tourists, it still holds a secret or two. This bustling market is a treasure trove of independent stalls selling everything from vintage clothing to exotic spices, artisan goods, and locally sourced food. The real hidden gem is the array of street food vendors tucked inside the market halls, where you can sample authentic, homemade delicacies at very affordable prices.
- **Why It's a Hidden Gem**: While the market itself is well-known, the food offerings can sometimes fly under the radar. Locals know that St. Nicholas Market is the place to grab a quick and delicious bite while enjoying a lively atmosphere that showcases Bristol's vibrant cultural scene.

6. Ashton Court Estate

- **Location**: Ashton Court Estate, Long Ashton, Bristol BS41 9JN
- **Overview**: Just outside the city center, Ashton Court Estate offers a peaceful retreat with expansive grounds, woodlands, and meadows. It's a popular spot for picnics, walking, and cycling, but not as widely known to tourists as other green spaces in the city. The estate also hosts several events throughout the year, including the Bristol Balloon Fiesta. The expansive grounds are perfect for anyone looking to explore nature or get away from the city's hustle and bustle.
- **Why It's a Hidden Gem**: While locals flock to Ashton Court for outdoor activities and its stunning views of the city, it's

often overlooked by tourists in favor of more central attractions. The estate is large enough to offer space and serenity, even on a busy day.

7. The Arnolfini Café & Bookshop

- **Location**: 16 Narrow Quay, Bristol BS1 4QA
- **Overview**: The Arnolfini is one of Bristol's most renowned contemporary art galleries, but it also has a hidden gem in its café and bookshop. Set in a peaceful spot along the waterfront, the café serves delicious, locally sourced food, and the bookshop is a treasure trove of unique reads, from art to poetry. The space is a perfect place to relax, whether you want to enjoy a coffee with a view or immerse yourself in a great book.
- **Why It's a Hidden Gem**: While the Arnolfini gallery itself is popular, the café and bookshop are often overlooked by visitors who focus solely on the art exhibits. Locals know that this is a perfect place to unwind in a charming and quiet environment, away from the tourist crowds.

8. The Clifton Observatory and Camera Obscura

- **Location**: Clifton Down, Bristol BS8 3LT
- **Overview**: Perched high above the Avon Gorge, the Clifton Observatory offers one of the best views in the city. While most visitors flock to the nearby Clifton Suspension Bridge, the observatory is often quieter and less crowded. It houses a fascinating camera obscura, which allows visitors to view real-time images of the surrounding area. It's a unique way to experience the city's panoramic views, and the café at the top of the hill serves excellent homemade cakes and coffee.
- **Why It's a Hidden Gem**: Though the Clifton Suspension Bridge gets all the attention, the Clifton Observatory is a hidden gem that provides a more tranquil experience with stunning views, perfect for those who want to escape the crowds.

Bristol is a city full of surprises, and while it has some well-known attractions, the real charm lies in its hidden gems. From secret gardens and historic caves to quiet cafés and stunning viewpoints, the local treasures are waiting to be discovered. Venture off the beaten path, and you'll uncover a side of Bristol that few visitors get to experience. Whether you're a first-time traveler or a returning visitor, these hidden gems will give you a deeper appreciation of this eclectic and vibrant city.

ADVENTUROUS ACTIVITIES

Exploring the Avon Gorge and Clifton Suspension Bridge

Bristol's Avon Gorge and the iconic Clifton Suspension Bridge are among the city's most captivating natural and architectural wonders, offering visitors an exhilarating range of adventurous activities. Whether you're a thrill-seeker or a nature lover, the area provides an abundance of ways to explore its breathtaking beauty and rich history.

Overview of the Avon Gorge

The Avon Gorge, carved by the River Avon, offers some of the most spectacular views in Bristol. The dramatic cliffs that line the gorge rise sharply from the river below, creating an impressive natural landscape that contrasts beautifully with the city's urban surroundings. With sweeping views of the river, the Clifton Suspension Bridge, and the lush woodlands of Clifton Down, the gorge is a must-visit for anyone interested in outdoor exploration. For those seeking adventure, the area has an array of activities that make the most of its stunning geography.

1. Clifton Suspension Bridge: The Ultimate Landmark

- **Location**: Clifton, Bristol BS8 3PA
- **Overview**: Spanning the Avon Gorge, the Clifton Suspension Bridge is one of the most recognizable landmarks in Bristol. Designed by the famous engineer Isambard Kingdom Brunel, the bridge offers not only a glimpse into Victorian engineering but also some of the best vantage points in the city. Crossing the bridge on foot or by car gives you an up-close view of its striking design and offers spectacular views of the gorge and river below.
- **Adventurous Activity**: For the adventurous, the Clifton Suspension Bridge offers a unique experience of walking across this architectural marvel, taking in the panoramic vistas as you make your way from the Clifton side to the Leigh Woods side. The bridge is especially awe-inspiring during sunrise or sunset when the golden light bathes the landscape.

2. Hiking the Avon Gorge Trails

- **Location**: Avon Gorge, Clifton, Bristol
- **Overview**: The surrounding area of the Avon Gorge is crisscrossed with several scenic walking trails, perfect for hiking enthusiasts. The trails offer various levels of difficulty, from easy strolls to more challenging hikes. As you walk through the winding paths, you'll pass through woodlands, enjoy panoramic views of the gorge, and witness diverse wildlife, including peregrine falcons, which have made the cliffs their home.
- **Adventurous Activity**: The most popular trail, which runs along the edge of the gorge, provides breathtaking views of the Clifton Suspension Bridge as well as the beautiful River Avon. The journey offers plenty of opportunities for adventurers to pause and take in the surrounding views, with each turn offering a new perspective of the river and gorge. The hike can also be combined with a visit to the Clifton Observatory, located high on the cliffs, providing an ideal

spot for rest and photography.

3. Rock Climbing and Abseiling in Avon Gorge

- **Location**: Avon Gorge, Clifton, Bristol
- **Overview**: For those seeking a more adrenaline-fueled adventure, Avon Gorge is one of the premier locations for rock climbing and abseiling in the UK. The steep, dramatic cliffs provide an exciting challenge for climbers, with routes available for both beginners and seasoned climbers. The surrounding natural landscape adds to the thrill, with stunning views of the gorge and the city's skyline from the top.
- **Adventurous Activity**: Local adventure companies offer rock climbing and abseiling experiences, allowing you to scale the gorge's limestone cliffs or descend its heights. These experiences offer an unmatched sense of adventure, with expert guides ensuring safety while you enjoy the thrill of conquering the cliffs. Climbing offers not only physical challenges but also a sense of achievement as you take in the awe-inspiring views at the summit.

4. Kayaking on the River Avon

- **Location**: River Avon, under Clifton Suspension Bridge
- **Overview**: For a more aquatic adventure, kayaking on the River Avon offers a unique perspective of the Avon Gorge and Clifton Suspension Bridge. Paddling through the calm waters of the river allows you to see the natural beauty of the gorge from below, passing under the towering bridge and the steep cliffs on either side.
- **Adventurous Activity**: Several kayak rental companies offer equipment and guided tours, providing a safe and thrilling way to experience the river's surroundings. Paddling through the gorge allows you to get up close to the wildlife and enjoy the serenity of the river, all while having an adventurous day out on the water. In addition to kayaking, stand-up paddleboarding is also a popular activity in this area.

5. Paragliding Over the Gorge

- **Location**: Clifton Down and the Avon Gorge
- **Overview**: For the ultimate thrill, paragliding offers the chance to soar above the Avon Gorge and the Clifton Suspension Bridge. From high above, you can take in the spectacular landscape, with sweeping views of the city and river. This activity is perfect for those looking to experience the gorge in a completely unique way.
- **Adventurous Activity**: Experienced instructors provide tandem flights, making it accessible even to beginners. As you glide through the air, you'll enjoy unparalleled views of the Clifton Suspension Bridge and the surrounding countryside. Paragliding offers an adrenaline rush while allowing you to take in the incredible natural beauty from a bird's-eye view.

6. The Clifton Observatory and Camera Obscura

- **Location**: Clifton Down, Bristol BS8 3LT
- **Overview**: Located atop the Avon Gorge, the Clifton Observatory offers sweeping panoramic views of the gorge and the Clifton Suspension Bridge. The observatory also houses a camera obscura, a fascinating optical device that projects live images of the surrounding landscape onto a surface inside the building.
- **Adventurous Activity**: While the experience at the observatory itself is more tranquil, it's the perfect spot to take in the awe-inspiring beauty of the gorge and the bridge from above. Afterward, you can enjoy a peaceful walk through the nearby Clifton Down or visit the café for a relaxing break.

Exploring the Avon Gorge and Clifton Suspension Bridge is a must-do for adventure enthusiasts visiting Bristol. With a wide range of activities—from hiking and rock climbing to kayaking and paragliding—the gorge offers something for everyone, no matter their level of adventure. The combination of natural beauty, history, and thrilling outdoor experiences makes it one of the best places in

Bristol to enjoy the great outdoors and push your limits. Whether you're looking for a peaceful hike or an adrenaline-packed challenge, the Avon Gorge provides the perfect setting to make unforgettable memories.

Kayaking and Paddleboarding in Bristol Harbour

Bristol Harbour, with its historic waterfront and vibrant atmosphere, is one of the city's most dynamic locations for outdoor adventure. The area offers a unique opportunity to explore the heart of Bristol from the water, with kayaking and paddleboarding being two of the most popular ways to enjoy the harbour. These activities allow visitors to experience the city's scenic beauty, its rich maritime history, and the serenity of its waters—all from a different perspective.

Overview of Bristol Harbour

Bristol Harbour is a vibrant waterway nestled between the bustling city and its industrial past, with a rich maritime heritage that once fueled the city's trade. Today, the area has been revitalized, offering a mix of modern attractions, historic docks, museums, shops, and cafés. The tranquil waters of the harbour provide the perfect setting for water sports, and its well-maintained infrastructure makes it easy for visitors to access and enjoy.

1. Kayaking on Bristol Harbour

- **Location**: Bristol Harbour, Wapping Wharf, BS1 4RN
- **Overview**: Kayaking in Bristol Harbour offers a tranquil yet adventurous way to explore the city's waterfront. Whether you're a seasoned paddler or a beginner, the calm waters of the harbour make it an ideal place to glide through the water, taking in the views of Bristol's landmarks, the floating docks,

and the surrounding buildings. The harbour is spacious, making it perfect for solo paddlers or groups, and allows kayakers to paddle at their own pace, whether they prefer a gentle excursion or a more intense workout.
- **Adventurous Activity**: Visitors can rent kayaks from local operators, who provide both single and tandem kayaks for hire. Many rental companies offer guided tours, which allow you to discover Bristol's waterfront in depth, learn about its history, and explore hidden spots along the water. Paddling along the harbour, you can expect views of iconic landmarks such as the SS Great Britain, the M Shed, and the historic docks. The calm waters of the harbour are ideal for leisurely exploration, offering a peaceful escape from the city's hustle and bustle.
- **Cost**: Kayak rental prices typically range from £15-£25 for a 1-hour rental, with guided tours available for around £30-£40 per person.

2. Paddleboarding on Bristol Harbour

- **Location**: Bristol Harbour, Wapping Wharf, BS1 4RN
- **Overview**: Stand-up paddleboarding (SUP) has become increasingly popular in Bristol, offering an exciting and relaxing way to experience the harbour. Paddleboarding allows you to stand on a large board and use a paddle to glide through the water. Bristol Harbour is an excellent spot for both beginners and more experienced paddleboarders, as the waters are generally calm and the area offers plenty of space to explore.
- **Adventurous Activity**: Paddleboarding in the harbour gives you the chance to take in stunning views of the city skyline and its historical landmarks from the water. Whether you prefer a calm paddle around the floating docks or a more invigorating route closer to the open water, there's plenty of opportunity for adventure. SUP is also a fantastic full-body workout, combining balance, strength, and core stability. For those new to the activity, local companies offer introductory lessons and group sessions to ensure you feel confident

before venturing out on your own.
- **Cost**: Rental prices for paddleboards are usually around £20-£30 for a 1-hour rental, with lessons or group sessions priced at around £35-£45 per person.

Guided Tours and Experiences

- **Location**: Bristol Harbour
- **Overview**: For those seeking a more immersive and informative experience, several operators offer guided kayaking and paddleboarding tours around the harbour. These tours are led by experienced instructors who not only provide safety tips but also share local history, hidden gems, and insights into Bristol's maritime legacy. Guided tours are an excellent way to explore the city's waterfront without worrying about navigation, and they allow you to discover areas of the harbour that you might not find on your own.
- **Adventurous Activity**: On these tours, you can learn about the significance of Bristol's docks, the importance of the River Avon in the city's development, and the famous vessels such as the SS Great Britain. As you paddle along the river, you'll be treated to stunning views of Bristol's landmarks, such as the Wills Memorial Building and the Bristol Cathedral, from a unique perspective.
- **Cost**: Guided tours typically range from £30-£50 per person, depending on the duration and type of tour (e.g., sunset tours or historical tours).

Seasonal Activities and Events

- **Location**: Bristol Harbour
- **Overview**: Throughout the year, Bristol Harbour hosts various events and seasonal activities that incorporate kayaking and paddleboarding. These include special races, water festivals, and community events where participants can enjoy friendly competitions or simply join in the fun. The harbour is also home to seasonal rental services that cater to adventurers throughout the year, with additional events

planned for the summer months, such as sunset paddleboarding sessions, moonlight kayaking, and even Christmas-themed water activities.
- **Adventurous Activity**: During these events, you can engage in unique activities like synchronized paddleboarding, group races, or themed water tours, all while enjoying the festive atmosphere of the harbour. Whether you're paddling through the calm evening waters or joining a lively event, these activities offer a social and adventurous way to enjoy Bristol's waterfront.
- **Cost**: Event participation prices vary, typically starting from £15-£20 per person for individual events.

Night-Time Paddleboarding and Kayaking

- **Location**: Bristol Harbour
- **Overview**: For an unforgettable experience, why not try paddleboarding or kayaking at night? Several operators in Bristol offer night-time paddleboarding and kayaking experiences, where participants venture out on the water under the stars, illuminated by the city's twinkling lights. The calm waters of the harbour create a serene and tranquil atmosphere, making this a unique way to experience Bristol's waterfront after dark.
- **Adventurous Activity**: Night-time kayaking or paddleboarding adds an extra layer of excitement and adventure, as the city's buildings and landmarks take on a new life when lit up. These nocturnal excursions often include the added thrill of navigating under the Clifton Suspension Bridge or gliding past the illuminated SS Great Britain, creating an atmosphere of wonder and discovery.
- **Cost**: Night-time rentals or guided tours are priced around £25-£40 per person, depending on the duration of the experience.

Kayaking and paddleboarding in Bristol Harbour offer an ideal way to engage with the city's stunning waterfront while enjoying a mix of adventure, relaxation, and sightseeing. Whether you're paddling under the famous Clifton Suspension Bridge, joining a guided tour to uncover the city's maritime past, or simply enjoying the serenity of the water, Bristol Harbour provides a variety of ways to explore. With rental options available year-round and a range of activities for all levels of experience, it's the perfect setting for outdoor enthusiasts seeking a unique perspective of this vibrant city.

Hot Air Balloon Rides: A Sky-High View of the City

For an unforgettable, breathtaking experience in Bristol, hot air balloon rides offer a unique opportunity to soar high above the city and enjoy its stunning landscapes from the sky. Whether you're looking for an exhilarating adventure or a peaceful, serene experience, taking a hot air balloon ride in Bristol provides a bird's-eye view of the city's iconic landmarks, green hills, and the meandering River Avon.

Overview of Hot Air Ballooning in Bristol

Bristol is renowned for its connection to ballooning, being home to one of the most famous ballooning events in the world—the Bristol International Balloon Fiesta. Every August, hundreds of hot air balloons fill the sky over the city, creating a vibrant spectacle. However, hot air balloon rides in Bristol are not limited to this annual event. They are available throughout the year, offering residents and visitors alike a chance to take in spectacular views of the city's historic skyline, the surrounding countryside, and the scenic Avon Gorge, all from an elevated perspective.

1. Scenic Balloon Rides Over Bristol

- **Location**: Various launch sites around Bristol, including Ashton Court Estate and other scenic spots in the surrounding countryside.

- **Overview**: Hot air balloon rides in Bristol typically take off from locations just outside the city center, offering a tranquil escape as you rise above the bustling streets below. Once in the air, passengers can take in sweeping views of the city's landmarks, including the Clifton Suspension Bridge, the SS Great Britain, and the lush green parks that dot the area. The beauty of ballooning lies in the leisurely pace; you'll glide through the sky, free from the noise of the world, while absorbing the stunning views. The ride generally lasts between 45 minutes to 1 hour, depending on weather conditions and the flight path chosen by the pilot.
- **Adventurous Activity**: The thrill of ascending into the sky and gently floating with the wind is unlike any other. The sense of peace and tranquility that comes from being so high up is unmatched, and the views of Bristol's iconic architecture, combined with the natural beauty of the surrounding countryside, are mesmerizing. Ballooning offers a new perspective on the city, giving you a chance to see landmarks such as the River Avon snaking through the landscape and the picturesque rolling hills that surround the city.
- **Cost**: Prices for hot air balloon rides typically range from £120-£180 per person, depending on the time of year, the duration of the flight, and the ballooning company. Private or exclusive flights are also available for special occasions and can be more expensive, typically starting at £300 per person.

2. Sunrise and Sunset Balloon Rides

- **Location**: Launch points around Bristol, such as Ashton Court Estate or other scenic countryside areas.
- **Overview**: For an even more magical experience, you can opt for a sunrise or sunset hot air balloon ride. These early morning and late evening flights allow you to experience Bristol in the soft, golden light of the sun's rising or setting. As the sun casts its warm glow over the city, you'll enjoy breathtaking views of Bristol bathed in natural light, with the calm, early morning or evening air adding a sense of

tranquility to the experience.
- **Adventurous Activity**: The calmness of the morning or evening skies creates a serene atmosphere that makes these rides particularly special. Floating above the city as the first light of dawn breaks or while the last golden rays of the day set the sky alight is a memory you'll cherish forever. These rides also offer a quieter, more intimate experience, as there are fewer distractions and a sense of calm that enhances the feeling of adventure.
- **Cost**: Sunrise and sunset balloon rides are slightly more expensive due to their exclusivity and the timing of the flights, with prices typically ranging from £150-£250 per person.

3. Private and Exclusive Balloon Experiences

- **Location**: Various launch locations across Bristol and the surrounding countryside.
- **Overview**: For those looking for a truly luxurious and private experience, Bristol offers private hot air balloon rides, perfect for couples, families, or groups of friends. These rides are often tailored to your specific preferences, providing a more personalized and intimate experience. Some companies offer special packages for anniversaries, birthdays, and other celebrations, making the balloon ride even more memorable.
- **Adventurous Activity**: A private hot air balloon ride offers complete control over the experience. Whether you want a more relaxed pace or a specific route, the ride is yours to enjoy in a way that suits you best. With exclusive baskets, private pilots, and the ability to customize your itinerary, these rides provide an unparalleled experience. For those celebrating special moments, a champagne toast at the end of the flight is a luxurious and memorable touch.
- **Cost**: Private hot air balloon experiences are more expensive, with prices generally starting from £350-£500 per person for a personalized flight.

4. Ballooning Events and Festivals

- **Location**: Bristol International Balloon Fiesta at Ashton Court Estate.
- **Overview**: While Bristol's famous International Balloon Fiesta happens annually in August, the event is more than just a chance to watch balloons in the sky. You can actually participate in the event by booking a ticket for a tethered balloon ride. During the fiesta, visitors have the chance to take a short flight in a hot air balloon, enjoying the fantastic views over the city as the sky fills with color.
- **Adventurous Activity**: While tethered rides are shorter than traditional flights, they still offer a thrilling experience of being up in the air and viewing the city from above. The balloon fiesta is a fantastic way to witness the spectacle of hundreds of balloons taking off from a single location, as well as to enjoy live entertainment, food stalls, and family-friendly activities on the ground.
- **Cost**: Tethered rides during the festival typically cost around £20-£30 per person, but full flight experiences may cost significantly more.

5. Balloon Ride Photography and Packages

- **Location**: Various launch points around Bristol and the countryside.
- **Overview**: Many hot air ballooning companies offer packages that include professional photography services, allowing you to capture every moment of your flight from a unique vantage point. These packages often include a photo album or digital gallery to commemorate the special day. For anyone looking to make their hot air balloon ride even more memorable, adding professional photos is a fantastic way to preserve the experience.
- **Adventurous Activity**: As you glide through the skies, having a photographer on hand to capture stunning aerial shots of Bristol and its surroundings is a wonderful way to relive the adventure long after you land. Whether you're

celebrating a special occasion or simply want to remember your flight, these photo packages provide a lasting memory of your journey above the city.
- **Cost**: Photography packages can range from £50-£100 depending on the number of photos and the type of package chosen.

Hot air balloon rides in Bristol are a must-try adventurous activity for anyone looking to experience the city in a truly unique and thrilling way. Whether you're gliding over the city at sunrise, enjoying a private flight with friends, or joining in the fun of the annual Bristol International Balloon Fiesta, these rides offer incredible views, a sense of serenity, and an unforgettable experience. If you're seeking an adventure that combines beauty, tranquility, and excitement, a hot air balloon ride over Bristol should definitely be on your bucket list.

ACCOMMODATIONS IN BRISTOL

Affordable Hostels and Budget Hotels in Bristol

Bristol, a vibrant city known for its rich history, stunning landmarks, and lively culture, is also home to a variety of budget-friendly accommodations. Whether you're a solo traveler, backpacker, or family looking for an affordable stay, Bristol offers plenty of options that don't compromise on comfort or convenience. Here is a carefully curated list of affordable hostels and budget hotels in Bristol, each providing a unique experience for those wanting to explore the city without breaking the bank.

1. YHA Bristol

- **Location**: The Glassboat, Welsh Back, Bristol BS1 4SB
- **Cost**: Dormitory beds from £20 per night; Private rooms from £55 per night
- **Overview**: Situated in a beautifully restored boat on the River Avon, YHA Bristol offers an affordable and unique place to stay. Located right in the heart of the city, it's a great

base for those wanting to explore the main attractions like the Bristol Cathedral, Queen Square, and the lively Harbourside area. The hostel offers both shared dorms and private rooms, making it ideal for solo travelers and groups alike. With a fully equipped kitchen, a cozy lounge area, and a bar, YHA Bristol is not only budget-friendly but also a social hub for travelers.

2. Bristol Backpackers Hostel

- **Location**: 57 New Bridewell, Bristol BS1 2QD
- **Cost**: Dormitory beds from £18 per night; Private rooms from £45 per night
- **Overview**: Bristol Backpackers Hostel is centrally located near many of the city's top attractions, including the famous Clifton Suspension Bridge and the SS Great Britain. This family-run hostel offers a relaxed, welcoming atmosphere for travelers of all kinds. Guests can enjoy a variety of amenities such as free Wi-Fi, luggage storage, and a communal kitchen. The hostel's laid-back vibe, combined with affordable pricing and prime location, makes it a popular choice for those seeking an economical yet comfortable stay in the city.

3. The Full Moon & Attic Bar

- **Location**: 1 North Street, Bristol BS3 1EN
- **Cost**: Dormitory beds from £15 per night; Private rooms from £50 per night
- **Overview**: Situated in the heart of Bristol's vibrant Southville area, The Full Moon & Attic Bar offers a unique hostel experience with a focus on affordable comfort. The hostel is above a popular pub and bar, making it an ideal spot for those looking to explore the city's nightlife. Guests can enjoy cozy dorm rooms, as well as private rooms for those seeking a little more privacy. The quirky atmosphere of the Full Moon, with its art-deco style and friendly staff, is perfect for socializing with fellow travelers, while the location provides

easy access to the city's attractions, including the Tobacco Factory and the Watershed.

4. Rock n Bowl Hostel

- **Location**: 2-3 Nelson Street, Bristol BS1 2HQ
- **Cost**: Dormitory beds from £17 per night; Private rooms from £45 per night
- **Overview**: Rock n Bowl Hostel offers a unique blend of fun and affordability in the heart of Bristol. Located just a short walk from the main shopping districts and cultural landmarks, this hostel is also home to an on-site bowling alley and a rock 'n' roll theme. Whether you're traveling solo or in a group, Rock n Bowl provides a lively atmosphere, complete with affordable rates and a range of fun activities. The hostel offers both dormitory and private rooms, with free Wi-Fi and access to a full-service kitchen. Its quirky and relaxed vibe makes it a great choice for travelers looking to mix affordability with entertainment.

5. Future Inn Bristol

- **Location**: Bond Street South, Bristol BS1 3EN
- **Cost**: Rooms from £65 per night
- **Overview**: If you're looking for a budget hotel that offers a bit more privacy and comfort, Future Inn Bristol is a great option. Located within walking distance from Bristol Temple Meads station and the city center, this hotel provides spacious and modern rooms at affordable rates. The rooms come with comfortable beds, an en-suite bathroom, flat-screen TVs, and tea/coffee-making facilities. Future Inn also has a restaurant on-site, offering guests a full English breakfast and a variety of meals. With a reputation for its clean, modern facilities and excellent value for money, Future Inn is an ideal choice for budget-conscious travelers seeking comfort.

6. The Cotham Arms Hotel

- **Location**: 57 Cotham Hill, Bristol BS6 6JY
- **Cost**: Rooms from £50 per night
- **Overview**: The Cotham Arms Hotel, located in a charming Victorian building, offers budget accommodation with a cozy pub setting. Situated near the University of Bristol and only a short distance from the city center, this hotel is perfect for those who want a quiet yet convenient location. Rooms come with simple but comfortable furnishings, and the pub downstairs serves a range of delicious meals and drinks. The Cotham Arms Hotel is an excellent option for travelers seeking an affordable stay with the added benefit of a traditional British pub atmosphere.

7. Ibis Bristol Temple Meads Quay

- **Location**: Avon Street, Bristol BS2 0PS
- **Cost**: Rooms from £60 per night
- **Overview**: Located near the Temple Meads Railway Station, the Ibis Bristol Temple Meads Quay is a modern budget hotel offering convenient accommodation for those arriving by train. With a variety of room options, including family rooms and twin rooms, this hotel offers great value for money. Each room features comfortable beds, free Wi-Fi, and en-suite bathrooms, making it a popular choice for both short and long stays. The hotel's location is perfect for exploring the nearby areas of Bristol, including the popular Harbourside, Cabot Circus, and St. Nicholas Market. For an affordable, no-frills option with reliable service, Ibis is a solid choice.

8. The Old Market Assembly

- **Location**: 25 West Street, Bristol BS2 0DF
- **Cost**: Dormitory beds from £20 per night; Private rooms from £60 per night
- **Overview**: The Old Market Assembly offers a blend of affordable accommodation with a lively atmosphere. This

hostel is located in the vibrant Old Market area, close to numerous pubs, bars, and restaurants. The hostel's rooms are clean and comfortable, and the hostel also features a bar and music venue downstairs. Guests can enjoy affordable rates and a sociable environment with plenty of opportunities to meet fellow travelers. The Old Market Assembly is perfect for those looking to experience Bristol's nightlife while staying in a welcoming, budget-friendly setting.

9. Travelodge Bristol Central

- **Location**: 1-3 Prince Street, Bristol BS1 4PL
- **Cost**: Rooms from £55 per night
- **Overview**: Travelodge Bristol Central offers a convenient and affordable option for travelers looking for a straightforward stay. Located in the heart of Bristol, close to attractions such as the Bristol Old Vic and Queen Square, this hotel provides spacious rooms with modern amenities. Rooms are equipped with comfortable beds, flat-screen TVs, and en-suite bathrooms. Travelodge's central location makes it easy to explore the city's shops, restaurants, and cultural venues. With its affordable pricing and central location, Travelodge is a reliable choice for budget-conscious travelers seeking a simple yet comfortable place to stay.

Bristol offers a variety of budget-friendly accommodations, ranging from quirky hostels to affordable hotels, each providing comfort, convenience, and value for money. Whether you're a backpacker looking for a fun, social environment or a couple seeking an affordable hotel for a weekend getaway, Bristol has plenty of options to suit your needs. By choosing from this list of affordable hostels and budget hotels, you can enjoy a memorable stay in one of the UK's most vibrant cities without stretching your travel budget.

Mid-Range and Luxury Hotels in Bristol

For those who prefer a more luxurious experience or need a bit more comfort during their stay, Bristol offers an impressive selection of mid-range and luxury hotels. These accommodations combine stylish design with exceptional service, ensuring guests have a memorable and comfortable stay. Whether you're traveling for business or leisure, these hotels provide the perfect balance of quality and value.

1. Hotel du Vin & Bistro Bristol

- **Location**: The Sugar House, 15-16 Welsh Back, Bristol BS1 4RR
- **Cost**: Rooms from £120 per night
- **Overview**: Nestled along the scenic waterfront, Hotel du Vin & Bistro offers a chic, contemporary setting with a rustic twist. Situated in a beautifully restored sugar warehouse, the hotel blends modern luxury with historic charm. Each room is uniquely designed, featuring stylish furnishings, modern amenities, and comfortable beds. The in-house Bistro serves a delectable menu of classic French dishes and regional delicacies. This hotel is ideal for travelers seeking a relaxing stay in a central location, with easy access to the vibrant Harbourside, the historic city centre, and local attractions.

2. Bristol Marriott Royal Hotel

- **Location**: College Green, Bristol BS1 5TA
- **Cost**: Rooms from £140 per night
- **Overview**: A prestigious 5-star property located in the heart of Bristol, the Bristol Marriott Royal Hotel is perfect for those seeking a refined experience. The hotel boasts elegant Victorian architecture with a grandiose interior. It offers spacious rooms equipped with luxurious amenities such as flat-screen TVs, minibars, and high-speed internet. The

Marriott's on-site restaurant, The Cast Iron Grill, offers a delectable selection of international dishes, while the historic surroundings provide an unparalleled backdrop for events and business meetings. With its prime location, the hotel is steps away from key attractions such as the Bristol Cathedral, the University of Bristol, and the vibrant Park Street.

3. The Bristol Hotel

- **Location**: Prince Street, Bristol BS1 4QF
- **Cost**: Rooms from £110 per night
- **Overview**: Located at the iconic waterfront in the heart of Bristol, The Bristol Hotel offers an elegant yet comfortable environment. Featuring stunning views of the city's harbor, this stylish hotel blends classic design with modern amenities. Guests can enjoy contemporary rooms equipped with air-conditioning, large-screen TVs, and high-speed Wi-Fi. The hotel's River Grille restaurant serves a selection of locally sourced, seasonal dishes, and the chic lounge bar is perfect for unwinding after a day of exploring. The Bristol Hotel is a fantastic choice for those who want to experience a mix of luxury and convenience in a central location, with attractions like the M Shed Museum and the Clifton Suspension Bridge nearby.

4. Radisson Blu Hotel, Bristol

- **Location**: Broad Quay, Bristol BS1 4BY
- **Cost**: Rooms from £125 per night
- **Overview**: The Radisson Blu Hotel offers a modern and luxurious experience right by the waterfront. With its sleek, contemporary design, it's a perfect choice for both business and leisure travelers. The hotel offers rooms with stunning views over the city's harborside or the beautiful Park Street. The rooms are spacious and feature large beds, flat-screen TVs, and marble bathrooms. Guests can enjoy a wide range of amenities, including a fitness center, restaurant, and bar.

The Radisson Blu is conveniently located near shopping areas like Cabot Circus, and it's within walking distance of Bristol's iconic landmarks, such as the Bristol Museum & Art Gallery and the historic Old City.

5. The Francis Hotel Bristol

- **Location**: Queen Square, Bristol BS1 4NT
- **Cost**: Rooms from £135 per night
- **Overview**: Set in an elegant Georgian townhouse, The Francis Hotel Bristol offers a boutique-style stay in the heart of the city. The hotel's charming interior features period details and modern comforts. Each room is designed with chic, contemporary decor, including comfortable beds, modern bathrooms, and high-quality amenities. Guests can enjoy a variety of services, such as a 24-hour front desk, a fitness center, and an on-site bar. Located just a short walk from Bristol's historic district, guests can explore the local attractions, including the Bristol Old Vic Theatre, the picturesque Queen Square, and the nearby St. Nicholas Market.

6. Mercure Bristol Grand Hotel

- **Location**: Broad Street, Bristol BS1 2EL
- **Cost**: Rooms from £105 per night
- **Overview**: Housed in a charming 19th-century building, the Mercure Bristol Grand Hotel is a welcoming mid-range property that offers modern comfort in a historic setting. The hotel is well-known for its spacious rooms, some of which feature beautiful views of the surrounding city. The hotel's restaurant serves a wide variety of British and European dishes, while the bar is perfect for enjoying a drink in the evening. The Mercure is located close to Bristol's Old City, making it an excellent base for exploring attractions like the Bristol Cathedral, Cabot Tower, and the iconic Bristol Harbour. This hotel provides a blend of contemporary style and classic architecture for a memorable stay.

7. Paintworks Apartments

- **Location**: Paintworks, Arnos Vale, Bristol BS4 3EH
- **Cost**: Apartments from £110 per night
- **Overview**: For those seeking a more home-like experience during their stay, Paintworks Apartments offer stylish serviced apartments in the creative hub of Bristol. Located in the artsy Paintworks development, these fully equipped apartments provide the perfect balance between comfort and convenience. Each apartment features a fully fitted kitchen, spacious living areas, and modern amenities such as Wi-Fi and flat-screen TVs. The surrounding area is known for its eclectic mix of independent shops, cafes, and art galleries. Paintworks Apartments are an ideal choice for travelers seeking flexibility and a more personal experience in Bristol.

These mid-range and luxury accommodations in Bristol provide an excellent range of choices for travelers seeking comfort, convenience, and style. Whether you're visiting for a weekend getaway, a business trip, or a longer stay, these hotels promise to elevate your experience of this vibrant city.

Quirky Accommodation in Bristol: Boats, Cabins, and Boutique Stays

For travelers seeking a unique and memorable stay, Bristol offers an array of quirky accommodations that go beyond the typical hotel experience. From staying on a boat in the harbor to immersing yourself in boutique-style cabins, these unconventional options will ensure your visit is both comfortable and unforgettable. Here's a guide to some of the most distinctive places to stay in this vibrant city.

1. The Bristol Harbour Hotel & Spa (Boats)

- **Location**: Waterfront, 53-55 Corn Street, Bristol BS1 1HT
- **Cost**: Rooms from £130 per night
- **Overview**: The Bristol Harbour Hotel & Spa offers an unusual experience by blending luxury and history, with some rooms featuring direct views over the water. While the hotel itself is housed in a historic building, there are several boat-themed rooms that give the feel of staying on the water without having to leave the comfort of land. This boutique hotel offers plush amenities, a relaxing spa, and a stunning location overlooking the iconic Bristol Harbour. It's an ideal base for those who want to stay in a quirky setting while still enjoying the full luxury experience.

2. The Floating Lodge (Boat)

- **Location**: The Floating Lodge, Welsh Back, Bristol BS1 4SB
- **Cost**: Rooms from £120 per night
- **Overview**: As the name suggests, The Floating Lodge offers an incredible opportunity to sleep aboard a boat right on Bristol's picturesque waterfront. This floating hotel combines modern comfort with maritime charm, offering a serene and peaceful environment with stunning views of the harbor. Each lodge is spacious and well-equipped with all the comforts of home, including air conditioning, en-suite bathrooms, and Wi-Fi. The perfect option for those looking to embrace a nautical experience without sacrificing comfort, The Floating Lodge allows guests to wake up to the gentle sound of water and the beautiful Bristol skyline.

3. Cabot Circus Apartments (Cabins)

- **Location**: Cabot Circus, Bristol BS1 3BX
- **Cost**: Apartments from £90 per night
- **Overview**: For a cozy and unique twist on traditional accommodation, the Cabot Circus Apartments offer a selection of quirky cabins located near Bristol's thriving shopping district. These creatively designed apartments are a great mix of comfort and style, featuring eclectic interior

designs with bold colors and rustic touches. You can enjoy the privacy of your own space while being just a short walk away from some of Bristol's best restaurants, shops, and attractions. Perfect for those who want something out of the ordinary, these cabins offer both the charm of a cabin stay and the convenience of urban amenities.

4. The White Lion House (Boutique Stay)

- **Location**: 6-7 The Mall, Clifton, Bristol BS8 4DR
- **Cost**: Rooms from £150 per night
- **Overview**: Situated in the stylish neighborhood of Clifton, The White Lion House is a boutique accommodation that perfectly combines charm, luxury, and a personal touch. This quirky hotel is located in a beautifully restored Georgian townhouse, offering uniquely decorated rooms with a vintage flair. Each room is individually styled with elegant furniture, antique features, and modern comforts. Guests can enjoy panoramic views of the Clifton Suspension Bridge and the picturesque Clifton Village. This boutique stay offers a calm, intimate atmosphere ideal for those looking for something with personality and history in a trendy area of Bristol.

5. The Mud Dock (Boutique Stay and Boat)

- **Location**: 3-4 The Grove, Bristol BS1 4RB
- **Cost**: Rooms from £100 per night
- **Overview**: For a stay that's a little different, The Mud Dock offers a blend of boutique accommodation and a waterside cafe in one of Bristol's most unique locations. Guests can choose to stay in rooms above the Mud Dock Café & Bicycle Workshop or on a converted boat moored by the docks. The rooms offer minimalist yet stylish interiors with modern amenities, while the cafe downstairs is a local favorite for enjoying delicious food with views of the harbor. This quirky spot is perfect for those who enjoy a laid-back vibe combined with unique lodging options. The Mud Dock is ideal for visitors wanting a blend of creativity, comfort, and local

charm in the heart of Bristol's harborside.

6. The Folk House (Boutique Stay)

- **Location**: 40a Park Street, Bristol BS1 5JG
- **Cost**: Rooms from £75 per night
- **Overview**: Nestled within the artistic district of Bristol, The Folk House offers a quirky, affordable boutique stay for travelers who want to explore the cultural side of the city. Housed in a charming Victorian building, The Folk House blends artsy decor with cozy accommodations. The rooms are stylishly decorated with vintage touches, and the property also hosts a café that serves locally sourced food and coffee. This boutique stay is perfect for those looking to experience Bristol's creative community and discover hidden gems like independent galleries, street art, and music venues.

7. The Beer Garden Cabin (Cabin)

- **Location**: St. Philips, Bristol BS2 0BH
- **Cost**: Rooms from £85 per night
- **Overview**: For a true offbeat experience, The Beer Garden Cabin offers quirky cabin-style accommodation on the outskirts of Bristol. This charming little cabin is tucked away in a peaceful spot, offering guests a quiet retreat with easy access to the city center. The Beer Garden Cabin is ideal for visitors who enjoy a rustic, homey feel. The cabin is small but comfortable, featuring basic amenities and a cozy atmosphere. It's the perfect option for those who want to experience the city in a different way, with a laid-back, countryside vibe combined with urban convenience.

8. The Old City Hostel (Boutique Hostel)

- **Location**: 33-35 High Street, Bristol BS1 2AZ
- **Cost**: Beds from £20 per night, Private Rooms from £60 per night

- **Overview**: The Old City Hostel is a quirky boutique hostel that blends traditional hostel-style accommodation with modern, unique features. Located in the heart of Bristol's Old City, this spot is a great choice for travelers looking for budget-friendly but charming lodging. The hostel offers a mix of dormitory beds and private rooms, all designed with creativity and comfort in mind. The location makes it easy to explore nearby attractions like St. Nicholas Market, Bristol Cathedral, and the Bristol Old Vic Theatre. It's a fantastic option for those seeking an affordable yet stylish place to stay with a social atmosphere.

Bristol offers a diverse selection of quirky accommodations that appeal to travelers seeking something truly unique. Whether you prefer a stay on the water, in a boutique cabin, or in an artistic and creative environment, Bristol has something to match your adventurous spirit. These quirky stays combine character, comfort, and the charm of one of England's most vibrant cities.

Bristol's Best Resorts: Luxury Escapes

Bristol offers a selection of luxurious resorts that cater to those seeking an indulgent and relaxing escape. These resorts provide a blend of exceptional service, upscale amenities, and stunning surroundings, ensuring that your stay in Bristol is as comfortable and unforgettable as possible. Here are some of the best resorts in and around Bristol, offering top-tier experiences for travelers looking for a lavish retreat.

1. The Bristol Harbour Hotel & Spa

- **Location**: Anchor Road, Bristol, BS1 5TJ
- **Average Price**: £180 - £350 per night
- **Overview**: Situated in the heart of Bristol, the Bristol Harbour

Hotel & Spa is a luxury resort that combines modern comfort with elegant décor. Located by the historic Bristol Harbour, this five-star resort is renowned for its stunning spa facilities, which include a relaxation area, a hydrotherapy pool, and a range of beauty treatments. Guests can also enjoy fine dining at The Jetty restaurant, offering fresh seafood and locally-sourced produce. The hotel's stylish rooms come with contemporary furnishings, luxury bathrooms, and views of the city or the water.

2. The Redcliffe Hotel & Spa

- **Location**: 7 Redcliffe Parade West, Bristol, BS1 6TX
- **Average Price**: £150 - £300 per night
- **Overview**: The Redcliffe Hotel & Spa is an upscale property offering a refined atmosphere and a prime location near Bristol's historic waterfront. The hotel's stylish rooms feature modern amenities, and many boast stunning views of the river. The full-service spa provides an array of rejuvenating treatments, while the on-site restaurant serves an exquisite selection of dishes made from local ingredients. The Redcliffe Hotel is an ideal choice for both relaxation and exploration, with attractions like the Bristol Aquarium and the SS Great Britain just a short walk away.

3. Aztec Hotel & Spa

- **Location**: Aztec West, Almondsbury, Bristol, BS32 4TS
- **Average Price**: £120 - £250 per night
- **Overview**: Located just outside of central Bristol, Aztec Hotel & Spa is a luxury retreat that combines a tranquil environment with easy access to the city center. This four-star resort offers a range of elegant rooms and suites, perfect for a relaxing getaway. The spa is one of the resort's highlights, featuring an indoor pool, sauna, steam room, and an extensive treatment menu. Guests can unwind in the contemporary surroundings, dine at the restaurant, or enjoy cocktails in the chic bar area. The resort is surrounded by

scenic gardens, making it an ideal place for those seeking peace and privacy.

4. The Lord Byron Hotel

- **Location**: 73 Waverley Road, Bristol, BS6 6LX
- **Average Price**: £100 - £225 per night
- **Overview**: The Lord Byron Hotel is an upscale, boutique hotel situated in the beautiful Clifton area of Bristol. Known for its luxurious rooms and intimate, friendly service, this hotel offers a warm and welcoming atmosphere. The hotel's refined design is inspired by its Victorian roots, featuring traditional architecture mixed with modern comforts. The Lord Byron offers access to exclusive, private gardens, ideal for a peaceful retreat. It's perfect for those wanting to explore Clifton's local attractions, such as the Clifton Suspension Bridge, just a short distance away.

5. Coombe Lodge

- **Location**: Blagdon, Bristol, BS40 7RE
- **Average Price**: £200 - £500 per night
- **Overview**: For a more secluded luxury experience, Coombe Lodge offers guests a truly unique getaway. Situated in the heart of the Somerset countryside, this stunning Georgian mansion is perfect for those looking for a luxurious rural retreat. The estate offers scenic views, private gardens, and a selection of luxury rooms. Coombe Lodge also features an award-winning spa and a fine-dining restaurant. It's an excellent choice for those seeking privacy, tranquillity, and first-class service, making it ideal for romantic getaways or small groups looking for exclusivity.

6. Hotel du Vin & Bistro

- **Location**: The Sugar House, 17-19 Welsh Back, Bristol, BS1 4RR
- **Average Price**: £130 - £280 per night

- **Overview**: Hotel du Vin & Bistro is a stylish, boutique resort located right on the Bristol Harbour, offering a cozy yet luxurious atmosphere. This hotel blends contemporary décor with traditional charm, providing guests with chic rooms that feature plush furnishings, luxurious bedding, and modern bathrooms. The on-site Bistro offers exceptional food, focusing on seasonal and locally sourced produce, while the vibrant bar serves a selection of cocktails and wines. Guests can unwind in the comfortable lounge areas or explore the nearby attractions along the waterfront, such as the M Shed museum and the Bristol Ferry Boat.

7. Lucknam Park Hotel & Spa

- **Location**: Colerne, Near Bath, Bristol, SN14 8AZ
- **Average Price**: £300 - £700 per night
- **Overview**: Located a short distance from Bristol, in the countryside near Bath, Lucknam Park Hotel & Spa offers the epitome of luxury. Set within 500 acres of parkland, the hotel is housed in a historic mansion and features a Michelin-starred restaurant, a world-class spa, and a range of outdoor activities such as horseback riding and archery. The rooms and suites are spacious, beautifully furnished, and equipped with all the comforts of modern living. Guests can indulge in the spa's treatments, enjoy gourmet dining, or take part in activities like cycling or tennis. This luxurious resort is the perfect choice for those looking to combine opulence with an escape from the city.

Bristol offers a variety of luxurious resorts that cater to different tastes and preferences, from urban hotels with spa facilities to tranquil countryside estates. Whether you're looking for a chic hotel by the waterfront or a grand retreat in the countryside, these resorts provide the perfect setting for an indulgent stay in one of England's most vibrant cities.

TOP ATTRACTIONS IN BRISTOL

Iconic Landmarks: Clifton Suspension Bridge and Bristol Cathedral

Bristol, a city that beautifully marries history, culture, and stunning architecture, is home to some of the UK's most iconic landmarks. Two of the most celebrated sights in the city are the **Clifton Suspension Bridge** and the **Bristol Cathedral**—both stand as proud symbols of Bristol's rich heritage and architectural marvels. Exploring these landmarks will not only immerse you in the city's historical charm but also offer breathtaking views and unforgettable experiences.

Clifton Suspension Bridge: A Marvel of Engineering and Design

Location: Clifton, Bristol
 How to Get There:
  The Clifton Suspension Bridge is located in the picturesque suburb of Clifton, which is a short bus ride or 15-minute walk from the city center. If you're feeling adventurous, consider walking up through

the leafy streets of Clifton Village, where you'll encounter boutique shops, quaint cafés, and stunning Georgian architecture as you make your way to the bridge.

The Experience:
As you approach the **Clifton Suspension Bridge**, the majestic sight of the bridge against the backdrop of the Avon Gorge is nothing short of awe-inspiring. Designed by the famous engineer **Isambard Kingdom Brunel**, the bridge was completed in 1864 and stands as a testament to Victorian engineering. Spanning the Avon Gorge and connecting Clifton to Leigh Woods, the bridge offers a unique perspective of Bristol and its surrounding areas.

Walking across the bridge, you'll feel the cool breeze from the gorge below and marvel at the views that stretch for miles across the city. The sweeping vistas of the River Avon, lush greenery, and the rolling hills of the surrounding countryside provide a tranquil setting that contrasts with the bustling city below.

At the **Clifton Suspension Bridge Visitor Centre**, located near the entrance, you can learn more about the bridge's fascinating history through interactive exhibits and displays. The centre offers a deep dive into the engineering ingenuity that brought this landmark to life, showcasing Brunel's vision and the challenges faced during its construction.

What You'll See on the Way:
As you stroll toward the bridge, you'll pass through **Clifton Village**, a charming area known for its elegant Georgian terraces and vibrant independent shops. Along the way, make sure to stop at **Clifton Down**, a large open space perfect for picnics and a relaxing break before crossing the bridge. If you're lucky, you might even catch sight of hot air balloons in the air, as the area is a popular spot for ballooning.

The bridge is most striking at sunset when the sky bathes the entire gorge in golden hues, creating an Instagram-worthy scene that will stay with you long after your visit.

Bristol Cathedral

Location: College Green, Bristol

How to Get There:
From the Clifton Suspension Bridge, take a leisurely 25-minute walk through the city center to reach the **Bristol Cathedral**. As you make your way, you'll pass through the vibrant streets of Bristol, filled with cultural landmarks and bustling cafes, offering a lovely transition from one landmark to the other.

The Experience:
The **Bristol Cathedral**, also known as the **Cathedral Church of the Holy and Undivided Trinity**, is a magnificent example of English Gothic architecture. This 12th-century cathedral is renowned for its stunning fan-vaulted ceilings, intricate stained-glass windows, and peaceful cloisters that transport visitors back in time.

Entering the cathedral, you'll immediately be struck by the soaring arches and the sense of grandeur that fills the space. The serene atmosphere, punctuated by the soft glow of light filtering through the stained glass, invites reflection and admiration. The **quire**, with its exquisitely detailed woodwork, is a highlight, and the cathedral's intricate stone carvings tell stories from the Bible and the city's history.

The cathedral is still an active place of worship, and you may be lucky enough to attend one of the regular services or organ recitals. If you visit during one of these occasions, the choir's beautiful hymns and the organ's resonant tones add to the cathedral's spiritual ambiance.

What You'll See on the Way:
As you approach the cathedral from College Green, you'll pass the historic **College Green Park**, a lovely open space that often hosts outdoor events and performances. The park offers a peaceful setting with views of the cathedral's impressive façade, making it the perfect spot for a moment of rest or to take in the surrounding architecture before entering the cathedral.

Unique Features:
One of the cathedral's unique features is its **West Front**, which faces College Green. The facade is adorned with numerous carvings of Biblical figures, which are an impressive sight up close. The **chapter house** and the **cloisters** are equally fascinating and offer a sense of tranquility, perfect for taking a quiet stroll or enjoying the beautiful surroundings.

Combining Both Landmarks

Both the **Clifton Suspension Bridge** and the **Bristol Cathedral** are must-see attractions for anyone visiting the city. They represent two different eras of Bristol's architectural history: one as a feat of industrial engineering, and the other as a monument to medieval and Gothic craftsmanship. Yet, they share a common thread of beauty and significance, both telling the story of Bristol's rich heritage.

By visiting these two landmarks, you'll have the chance to experience the best of both worlds—the stunning views and engineering brilliance of the Clifton Suspension Bridge and the awe-inspiring beauty and historical significance of Bristol Cathedral. The two sites are easily accessible from one another, making it possible to visit both in one day and gain a deeper appreciation for the architectural wonders that define Bristol.

Whether you're a history enthusiast, an architecture lover, or simply someone seeking breathtaking views and peace, the **Clifton Suspension Bridge** and **Bristol Cathedral** offer experiences that are both memorable and enriching. The walk between these two landmarks is as much a journey through Bristol's past as it is an exploration of the city's enduring beauty.

Bristol's Vibrant Street Art Scene: The Banksy Connection

Location: Various locations around Bristol
How to Get There:
Bristol's vibrant street art can be found throughout the city, but the **Banksy connection** is one of the most intriguing and widely celebrated aspects of this urban art form. To explore the street art scene, start your journey in the **Stokes Croft** and **Easton** neighborhoods, both of which are known for their walls covered in murals and graffiti that have transformed the cityscape into an outdoor gallery. **Stokes Croft** is about a 20-minute walk from the city center, and **Easton** is a short bus ride or 25-minute walk away.

As you walk through the streets of these neighborhoods, you'll be greeted by vibrant, larger-than-life works of art, some of which are recognized as having been created by **Banksy**, the elusive, globally famous street artist. While Banksy's works can be found scattered throughout the city, the area around **Stokes Croft** is often regarded as his creative home base.

The Experience:
Walking through these neighborhoods is like stepping into an open-air gallery, where the walls themselves tell a story of political, social, and cultural messages. **Banksy**, whose identity remains unknown, has left his mark on Bristol with pieces that challenge the status quo, question societal norms, and often add a humorous touch to serious topics.

One of the most famous Banksy works in the city is **"The Girl with the Pierced Eardrum"**, located on the side of a house in the **Stokes Croft** area. This piece, a reimagining of Vermeer's classic painting, features a girl with a pearl earring—only now, the earring is a security alarm. This playful yet thought-provoking artwork embodies Banksy's signature style, blending classic art with contemporary commentary.

Other notable pieces include **"The Mild Mild West"**, which depicts a teddy bear throwing a Molotov cocktail, and **"Well Hung Lover"**, a cheeky and controversial piece located on the side of a house in the **Southville** area. As you wander through these areas, be sure to look up, down, and all around—you never know what hidden gems you'll find tucked away in unexpected corners of the city.

What You'll See on the Way:
While exploring the street art, you'll pass by **Stokes Croft**, which is home to vibrant cafes, quirky boutiques, and the iconic **Croft Ales Brewery**. Grab a coffee or a pint at one of the local spots to fully immerse yourself in the atmosphere of this creative neighborhood.

Make sure to stop by **The People's Republic of Stokes Croft**, a cultural hub that hosts art exhibitions, music events, and political activism. Here, the message of street art is taken to heart, and you'll find a space that celebrates the intersection of art, activism, and community.

The Impact of Banksy on Bristol's Art Culture

Bristol has long been regarded as a hotbed for street art, but the influence of **Banksy** has catapulted the city into the international spotlight. His work has inspired countless artists to experiment with urban spaces, and the city's relationship with street art has become an integral part of its identity.

Walking through **Bristol's street art scene**, you'll notice how much the community values creativity and expression. Public murals are celebrated, and many local businesses support the artistic movement by displaying works by up-and-coming artists alongside well-known pieces. The influence of Banksy has also led to the development of a number of street art festivals, such as **Upfest**, Europe's largest street art festival, which takes place annually in **South Bristol** and draws artists from around the world.

As you explore the streets, you'll notice how street art has evolved over the years in Bristol. It began as a form of rebellion and protest, but today it's an accepted and celebrated part of the city's artistic landscape. Many of the murals reflect political and social issues, adding layers of meaning to each piece and encouraging viewers to reflect on the world around them.

Bristol Museums and Galleries

Beyond street art, **Bristol's museums and art galleries** offer even more to explore. If you're looking to immerse yourself in the city's cultural history, make sure to visit the **Bristol Museum and Art Gallery**, located in **Queens Road**. This museum boasts an impressive collection of art, archaeology, and natural history. The art collection includes works by famous local artists such as **Sir John Tenniel**, who illustrated the famous **Alice's Adventures in Wonderland** books.

Just a short walk from the museum, you'll also find the **Arnolfini Gallery**, one of the UK's leading contemporary arts spaces. The gallery showcases cutting-edge exhibitions that challenge traditional notions of art, providing a perfect complement to Bristol's vibrant street art scene.

Why Bristol's Street Art Scene is Unique

Bristol's street art is more than just spray paint on a wall—it's an integral part of the city's artistic identity. It's the place where creativity is encouraged, and political and social messages are conveyed in an impactful and accessible way. From **Banksy** to the next generation of street artists, Bristol continues to evolve as a cultural hub where art is always evolving, challenging the norms, and offering a fresh perspective.

Exploring the **vibrant street art scene** is an unforgettable experience that allows you to not only witness some of the most famous and striking works of art in the world but also to step into the heart of Bristol's creative community. Whether you're a fan of Banksy's thought-provoking pieces or simply enjoy the energy and creativity of street art, Bristol's urban canvas offers something for everyone.

Plan Your Visit

- **When to Visit**: The best time to visit Bristol's street art scene is in the spring and summer when the city is buzzing with festivals and outdoor events. This is also the time when many new pieces are unveiled as part of various street art festivals.
- **Duration**: Plan to spend at least a few hours wandering through **Stokes Croft** and **Easton** to take in the full range of street art. For a deeper dive, join a street art walking tour led by local guides who can provide fascinating insights into the pieces and the artists behind them.
- **Entrance Fees**: Most of the street art is free to view, though guided tours may have a small fee. Bristol's art galleries and museums may also charge an entry fee, but many have free entry on certain days.

Whether you're exploring Bristol's famous street art or delving into the city's art galleries and museums, one thing is certain: the cultural journey you embark on will be one that challenges your perceptions, delights your senses, and immerses you in a city that lives and breathes creativity.

Museums and Art Galleries

Bristol, a city that hums with creativity and history, is a treasure trove of cultural gems that deserve to be explored at a leisurely pace. From the moment you step into the heart of this vibrant city, you'll be greeted by an inspiring blend of modern art, historic artifacts, and interactive exhibitions. Whether you're an art enthusiast, a history buff, or a curious traveler seeking to uncover the soul of Bristol, its museums and galleries offer a cultural journey that's as diverse and dynamic as the city itself.

Getting There:

Start your cultural journey in the **city center**, easily accessible by foot, bus, or tram. If you're coming by train, **Bristol Temple Meads** station is just a 20-minute walk away from many of the city's key attractions. As you step out of the station, you'll find yourself immersed in the bustling city streets, lined with architectural gems that are steeped in history. The **Bristol Museum and Art Gallery**, one of the most well-known institutions in the city, is located on **Queens Road**, just a 10-minute walk from the city center. On your way there, you'll pass through **Park Street**, a lively thoroughfare that boasts quirky shops, independent cafes, and historical buildings.

As you make your way to the museum, you'll notice how **Bristol's juxtaposition of old and new** creates a unique sense of place. The streets are lined with Georgian and Victorian buildings, their stately facades a reminder of the city's past, while the occasional mural or modern art piece reminds you that Bristol is a hub of contemporary creativity.

Bristol Museum and Art Gallery: A Journey Through Time and Art

Once you reach the **Bristol Museum and Art Gallery**, you'll be greeted by an imposing, yet welcoming, Victorian building with stone carvings and grand archways. This museum, which opened in 1823, is a testament to the city's commitment to preserving and showcasing its cultural heritage. The museum is home to an extensive collection that spans a variety of topics, from **ancient Egypt** to **contemporary art**, and features works from some of the world's most celebrated artists, including **John Tenniel**, the illustrator behind **Alice's Adventures in Wonderland**.

As you step inside, you'll first encounter the **archaeology galleries**, which house incredible artifacts from Bristol's Roman past, as well as **Egyptian mummies** and **medieval relics** that tell stories of the city's rich history. Moving through the museum, you'll discover exhibits dedicated to **geology**, **natural history**, and **European art**.

The art collection is particularly impressive, with works by artists like **Edward Burne-Jones** and **Banksy**, the infamous street artist whose work first gained recognition in Bristol.

One of the museum's highlights is the **temporary exhibitions**, which change regularly to showcase innovative works of contemporary artists and thought-provoking cultural exhibitions. These exhibits often feature local talent, providing a platform for the city's creative community to shine.

The Arnolfini: Contemporary Art at Its Best

A short walk from the **Bristol Museum and Art Gallery** brings you to the **Arnolfini**, a landmark in Bristol's contemporary art scene. Situated on the harborside, this modern art gallery is housed in a former warehouse and offers a striking contrast to the traditional museums of the city. The building itself is a work of art, with its industrial architecture and expansive glass windows overlooking the harbor.

Inside, the gallery features a rotating selection of contemporary art exhibitions, ranging from **painting** and **sculpture** to **film** and **performance art**. The **Arnolfini** is known for its boundary-pushing exhibitions, which challenge conventional ideas of art and provoke reflection on social, political, and cultural issues. Whether you're viewing a thought-provoking video installation or admiring an abstract painting, there's always something to ignite your creativity and stimulate your thinking.

In addition to its exhibitions, the **Arnolfini** hosts a variety of public events, including **art talks**, **workshops**, and **live performances**. Don't miss the **café** located within the gallery, where you can enjoy a coffee and take in the views of the harbor while reflecting on the art you've just experienced.

M Shed: Exploring Bristol's Industrial Past

Just a stone's throw from the **Arnolfini** is **M Shed**, a fascinating museum that focuses on Bristol's industrial heritage. Housed in a former dockside warehouse, **M Shed** explores the history of the city through its people, its industries, and its landmarks. The museum's exhibits delve into the city's role in **maritime trade**, **slavery**, **aviation**, and the **industrial revolution**, providing a comprehensive look at how Bristol became the dynamic city it is today.

One of the standout exhibits at **M Shed** is the **Bristol's World War II** display, which features photographs, artifacts, and stories from the wartime experiences of Bristol's residents. The museum's interactive exhibits make it an ideal stop for families and those interested in hands-on learning.

Bristol's Artistic Landscape: Beyond the Galleries

While museums and galleries provide a structured glimpse into Bristol's cultural landscape, the city's artistic spirit extends far beyond the walls of these institutions. Bristol's **street art** scene, in particular, is world-renowned, and much of it is located in the **Stokes Croft** area, a short bus ride or 20-minute walk from the museum district.

As you walk through the streets of **Stokes Croft** and the surrounding neighborhoods, you'll encounter colorful murals, graffiti, and installations created by local artists. One of the most famous contributions to this scene is **Banksy**, the anonymous street artist whose works have become synonymous with Bristol's creative identity. These outdoor artworks provide a unique, constantly changing canvas for Bristol's artistic community and make the city feel alive with creativity at every turn.

Make the Most of Your Cultural Journey

Bristol's museums and galleries offer a journey through time and art that's not to be missed. Whether you're marveling at ancient artifacts in the **Bristol Museum and Art Gallery**, admiring contemporary works at the **Arnolfini**, or exploring the industrial history of the city at **M Shed**, each stop on your cultural journey brings a new layer of understanding about this vibrant city.

To make the most of your visit, take your time exploring each museum and gallery at your own pace. Don't forget to check out the local café culture in between your visits, as Bristol's eclectic coffee shops and restaurants are the perfect place to relax and reflect on the art you've seen.

Tip: Many of the museums and galleries in Bristol offer free admission, but special exhibits and events may charge an entry fee. Be sure to check their websites for up-to-date information on opening hours and exhibition schedules.

Bristol's museums and art galleries provide an enriching cultural experience that showcases the city's commitment to preserving its heritage while embracing the creativity of its modern artists. As you explore, you'll gain a deeper appreciation for Bristol's dynamic past, present, and future, leaving you with a lasting connection to this truly unique city.

CURRENCY EXCHANGE

Local Currency: The Pound Sterling (£)

In Bristol, as with the rest of the United Kingdom, the official currency is the Pound Sterling (£). Known for its enduring legacy and symbol of economic strength, the pound is one of the oldest currencies still in use today, dating back over 1,200 years. For travelers, understanding and navigating the local currency is an essential step toward a seamless Bristol experience.

Understanding the Pound Sterling

The pound (£) is divided into 100 pence (p). Coins come in denominations of 1p, 2p, 5p, 10p, 20p, 50p, £1, and £2, while banknotes are issued in £5, £10, £20, and £50 denominations. Each coin and note showcases a piece of Britain's rich cultural and historical heritage, with portraits of Queen Elizabeth II (or King Charles III on newer designs) and famous landmarks or personalities gracing their surfaces.

Currency Exchange: A Simple Process

Exchanging your money into pounds is straightforward, with numerous options available in Bristol. Many travelers prefer the convenience of withdrawing cash directly from ATMs, which offer competitive exchange rates. Major credit and debit cards are widely accepted, including Visa, Mastercard, and American Express. However, carrying some cash is always advisable for small transactions at local markets or independent shops.

Where to Exchange Currency

1. **Banks and Currency Exchange Offices**
   Banks like HSBC, Barclays, and Lloyds Bank offer reliable currency exchange services during business hours, typically from 9:00 AM to 5:00 PM. For more flexibility, Travelex locations and independent exchange offices can be found in the city center, often with extended hours.

2. **Bristol Airport**
   If you're arriving at Bristol Airport, currency exchange kiosks are conveniently located in the arrivals and departures areas. While these may not offer the best rates, they're useful for exchanging small amounts on arrival.

3. **ATMs**
   ATMs are widespread across Bristol and accept most international cards. They provide competitive rates but check with your bank for any additional withdrawal fees. Look for machines affiliated with major networks like Visa Plus or Mastercard Cirrus for reliability.

4. **Post Offices**
   Many post offices in Bristol also provide currency exchange services, often with no commission fees. This can be a cost-effective option if you're staying near one.

Currency Tips for Travelers

- **Pay Contactless**: Most stores, cafes, and public transport systems in Bristol accept contactless payments. This is a quick and secure way to make purchases without handling

cash.
- **Be Aware of Exchange Fees**: If using a credit or debit card, opt to pay in pounds rather than your home currency to avoid dynamic currency conversion fees.
- **Check Rates Online**: Use apps or websites like XE.com to track live exchange rates and ensure you're getting the best deal.

Fun Fact: The Symbol of the Pound

The £ symbol originates from the Latin word "libra," meaning scales or balance. This reflects the pound's historical association with weight and measure, an apt metaphor for the city of Bristol, which has long balanced its historical charm with modern vibrancy.

Bristol's economy thrives on a blend of tradition and innovation, and its currency reflects this balance. Whether you're savoring a cup of coffee in an independent cafe, shopping for artisan goods at St Nicholas Market, or hopping on a ferry to explore the harbor, having a good understanding of the Pound Sterling ensures that you can fully enjoy every moment in this remarkable city.

Best Places to Exchange Currency in Bristol

Navigating currency exchange in a foreign city can feel like a daunting task, but Bristol offers a variety of convenient and traveler-friendly options to ensure you get the best value for your money. Whether you're arriving at the airport, strolling through the bustling city center, or preparing for your visit in advance, knowing where to exchange currency in Bristol can save you time and unnecessary costs.

1. Banks: Trusted and Secure Options

Banks like **HSBC**, **Barclays**, and **NatWest** are reliable choices for exchanging your currency. Located throughout the city, particularly in the city center, these institutions offer competitive exchange rates with low fees.

- **Location**: Broadmead, Clifton, and Cabot Circus have several branches conveniently situated for travelers.
- **Hours**: Typically open from 9:00 AM to 5:00 PM, Monday through Friday, with limited hours on Saturdays.
- **What to Expect**: Most banks require photo identification, and the process is straightforward. While banks may not always provide the highest rates, they offer security and transparency, which are invaluable for first-time visitors.

2. Currency Exchange Bureaus: Convenience with Flexibility

Specialized currency exchange offices like **Travelex** and local bureaus in Bristol cater to tourists looking for quick and hassle-free transactions. These can be found in prominent areas such as **Bristol Temple Meads Station** and **Broadmead Shopping Quarter**.

- **Why Choose Them**: These bureaus often offer more flexible operating hours, making them ideal for last-minute exchanges. However, it's worth comparing their rates as some may charge higher fees.
- **Pro Tip**: Look for signs advertising "no commission" deals to avoid hidden charges.

3. Bristol Airport: Exchange Before You Explore

If you prefer to have local currency in hand upon arrival, Bristol Airport offers several currency exchange kiosks, such as **Moneycorp**.

- **Convenience Factor**: Located in both arrivals and departures, these kiosks are easy to spot and provide an immediate solution.
- **What to Keep in Mind**: Airport rates tend to be less favorable, so exchange only a small amount here and plan

for better options in the city.

4. ATMs: Easy Access to Local Currency

ATMs are one of the simplest ways to access local currency in Bristol. Scattered across the city, particularly in high-traffic areas like **Cabot Circus**, **Harbourside**, and **Queen Square**, these machines accept most international cards.

- **Benefits**: ATMs typically offer better exchange rates than physical bureaus.
- **Fees**: Check with your bank regarding international withdrawal fees. Some local ATMs might add a small surcharge.
- **Tip for Travelers**: Look for ATMs connected to major banks like Lloyds or Santander to ensure reliability.

5. Post Offices: A Hidden Gem for Currency Exchange

Many travelers overlook post offices, but they're an excellent option for exchanging currency in Bristol. The **Bristol City Centre Post Office** on Baldwin Street is particularly convenient.

- **Why Post Offices?** They often provide competitive rates with minimal fees, and the process is straightforward.
- **Hours**: Generally open Monday through Saturday, with extended hours on weekdays.
- **Added Bonus**: Post offices are great for mailing postcards and picking up travel essentials, making them a multitasking haven for tourists.

Tips for a Smooth Currency Exchange Experience

- **Compare Rates**: Use apps like XE or Currency Converter to check real-time exchange rates before making a transaction.
- **Avoid Dynamic Conversion**: When paying with a card, always opt to pay in pounds (£) rather than your home currency to avoid additional fees.
- **Keep Small Bills Handy**: Having smaller denominations is

useful for tipping, local markets, and public transportation.

Bristol's vibrant mix of modern infrastructure and historical charm ensures that exchanging currency is a seamless part of your journey. Whether you're grabbing a pint at a cozy pub or shopping for artisanal goods at St Nicholas Market, having pounds in your pocket ensures you're ready to embrace all the city has to offer.

PACKING ESSENTIALS

Weekend Packing List: Light and Efficient

When planning a weekend trip, packing light is key to making the most of your time while avoiding the stress of overpacking. The goal is to bring only what you'll truly need, while ensuring you're prepared for all the activities you'll be enjoying. Here's your ultimate **weekend packing list** to help you stay efficient without sacrificing comfort or style.

1. Versatile Clothing

For a weekend getaway, your wardrobe should focus on versatility and comfort. Choose **outfits** that can easily be mixed and matched to suit a variety of activities, from casual sightseeing to a nice evening out.

- **2-3 Tops**: Opt for breathable materials like cotton or lightweight fabrics. A casual T-shirt, a button-up shirt for dinners, and a lightweight sweater or jacket for cooler evenings will cover most scenarios.
- **1 Pair of Jeans or Comfortable Pants**: A pair of jeans is usually the best go-to. It's versatile, stylish, and can be worn with almost anything.

- **1-2 Pairs of Shoes**: Depending on your activities, comfortable walking shoes are essential. If you plan to visit a fancy restaurant or attend an evening event, pack a pair of stylish yet comfortable shoes for those outings.
- **Light Jacket or Sweater**: A neutral-colored jacket that can be dressed up or down will be perfect for unpredictable weather. Look for a jacket that is water-resistant in case of rain, and pack a scarf if needed.

2. Toiletries: Travel-Sized and Compact

Packing toiletries efficiently means using smaller, travel-sized versions of your essentials to save space without compromising on personal hygiene.

- **Toothbrush, Toothpaste, and Floss**: These are the basics. Pack them in a small, leak-proof case to keep your bag organized.
- **Travel-Sized Shampoo and Conditioner**: Rather than lugging full-sized bottles, transfer your favorite shampoo and conditioner into smaller containers or use multi-purpose products.
- **Deodorant and Skincare Products**: A small deodorant and any skincare products you may need (moisturizer, sunscreen) should be included. Opt for a lightweight, hydrating moisturizer for weekend use.
- **Razor and Hairbrush**: A compact razor and a small hairbrush or comb will keep your grooming routine in check without taking up much space.

3. Electronics and Accessories

The right electronics can enhance your weekend trip without adding bulk to your luggage.

- **Smartphone and Charger**: Always have your phone charged and ready for navigation, photos, or communication. A portable charger can be invaluable if you'll be out exploring for long hours.

- **Headphones**: For moments when you want to unwind, pack a small pair of headphones or earbuds for music or podcasts.
- **Camera (Optional)**: If you're into photography, a compact camera or even your phone can capture the beauty of your destination without taking up much room.
- **Small Power Bank**: For those long days of sightseeing, having an extra charge can be a lifesaver, especially if you're using your phone for navigation or photos.

4. Travel Documents and Essentials

Ensure you have all the important travel documents organized and easily accessible.

- **ID and/or Passport**: Depending on your destination, make sure to carry identification or a passport.
- **Travel Itinerary**: A printed or digital version of your travel plans is always helpful for reference during your trip.
- **Credit Cards and Cash**: It's smart to have a small amount of cash on hand in case you visit places that don't accept cards. Keep your credit cards in a secure pocket or travel wallet.

5. Miscellaneous Essentials

There are a few additional items that will enhance your weekend getaway and ensure you're fully prepared for any situation.

- **Sunglasses**: Protect your eyes from the sun's glare while adding a stylish touch to your look.
- **Reusable Water Bottle**: Stay hydrated as you explore, and carry a lightweight, reusable water bottle to refill when needed.
- **Umbrella or Raincoat**: Depending on the weather forecast, a small travel umbrella or a foldable raincoat will keep you dry without adding much weight to your luggage.
- **Snacks**: A few granola bars or a small snack pack can help curb hunger during long walks or excursions.

6. A Small Daypack or Tote

For day trips, a small backpack or tote bag is essential. It's perfect for carrying your water bottle, camera, sunscreen, snacks, and anything else you need for the day. Look for a bag that's both functional and stylish, one that can be easily packed into your luggage when you're not using it.

Pro Tips for Efficient Packing:

- **Roll, Don't Fold**: Rolling your clothes instead of folding them helps save space and minimizes wrinkles.
- **Use Packing Cubes**: These nifty storage tools allow you to organize clothes, toiletries, and accessories, keeping everything compact and accessible.
- **Check the Weather**: Always check the weather forecast before packing to ensure you're bringing appropriate layers for your destination.
- **Leave Room for Souvenirs**: Leave some extra space in your bag in case you pick up a few souvenirs along the way.

By focusing on versatility, comfort, and a mix of practical items, you'll be able to pack light while being fully prepared for a memorable weekend adventure. With your essentials at hand, you'll be free to explore, unwind, and enjoy your getaway to the fullest!

Essentials for a 5-Day and 7-Day Bristol Trip

Packing for a 5-day or 7-day trip to Bristol requires a bit more foresight than a quick weekend getaway, but with the right essentials, you'll be ready for every adventure the city has to offer. Whether you're exploring historic landmarks, enjoying the local cuisine, or strolling through art galleries, your packing list should be practical, comfortable, and versatile. Here's a detailed guide to help you prepare for a smooth and enjoyable trip to this vibrant city.

1. Clothing: Layering for Comfort and Versatility

For a trip lasting 5 to 7 days, you'll want to pack versatile clothing that can be mixed and matched for different activities and changing weather. Bristol's climate can vary, so layering is key.

- **Tops**: Pack **5 to 7 tops**, including a mix of short-sleeve shirts, long-sleeve shirts, and perhaps a sweater or lightweight jacket. Bristol's weather can be unpredictable, so you may need layers to adjust to sudden temperature changes.
- **Bottoms**: Bring **2 to 3 pairs of pants** or **jeans** for daytime wear. Depending on your plans, consider packing **a pair of comfortable shorts** for warmer days and **a pair of dressier pants** for dinner or more formal outings.
- **Jacket and Outerwear**: Pack a **lightweight waterproof jacket** or a **windbreaker**, especially if visiting during the fall or spring. A **heavy coat** may be needed for winter months, but a packable jacket is a good choice if you prefer space-saving options.
- **Shoes**: For sightseeing, bring **comfortable walking shoes**. If you plan to explore Bristol's bustling streets or enjoy outdoor activities, a sturdy pair of sneakers will ensure comfort. For evenings out or a fancy dinner, pack **one pair of dress shoes** or stylish boots.
- **Accessories**: Depending on the weather, a **scarf**, **hat**, and **gloves** may be necessary, especially in colder months. Consider packing **sunglasses** for sunny days.

2. Toiletries: Essentials and Skin Care

You'll want to keep your toiletries simple yet comprehensive for a week-long trip. Opt for travel-sized versions of your skincare products, and focus on items that ensure comfort during your stay.

- **Toothbrush and Toothpaste**: Travel-sized versions are ideal. Keep these essentials in a compact toiletry bag to

maintain organization.
- **Shampoo, Conditioner, and Body Wash**: A small bottle of shampoo, conditioner, and body wash can last you through your trip. You may also want to pack a **multi-purpose bar soap** to save space.
- **Skincare Essentials**: If you're staying a week, you'll want to include your **moisturizer** and **sunscreen**. A good face sunscreen with SPF 30+ is essential, as Bristol has plenty of outdoor spaces to enjoy.
- **Razor, Deodorant, and Hairbrush**: Don't forget the basics! Pack a **razor**, **deodorant**, and a **compact hairbrush** to stay fresh and groomed.

3. Electronics: Stay Connected and Capture the Memories

While packing electronics for a longer trip, the focus should be on practicality. Choose compact gadgets that you'll actually use during your stay.

- **Smartphone and Charger**: Your phone is likely your main source for navigation, photos, and communication. Make sure you bring a **portable charger** as well, especially if you plan to explore all day.
- **Camera**: If you want to capture the stunning views of Bristol and its historic landmarks, pack a **compact digital camera** or simply use your phone for photos.
- **Power Adapter**: If you're traveling from abroad, remember to pack a **UK power adapter** to keep your devices charged.

4. Documents and Travel Essentials

Staying organized with your important documents ensures you can focus on enjoying the trip without any last-minute hassles.

- **Passport or ID**: For international travelers, keep your **passport** handy. If you're coming from within the UK, your ID will suffice, but make sure you have it accessible for check-in or entry to any sites.
- **Travel Insurance and Itinerary**: It's always a good idea to

have a copy of your **travel insurance policy**, emergency contacts, and your **trip itinerary** printed out.
- **Credit Cards and Cash**: While most places in Bristol accept card payments, keep some **cash** on hand for small purchases or in case of emergencies.
- **Public Transport Cards or Tickets**: If you plan to use the **Bristol public transport system**, having a **Bristol Ticket** or **Contactless Payment Card** can save you time and money.

5. Miscellaneous: Extras for Convenience

There are always small items that can make your trip easier and more enjoyable. Here's what you may want to consider bringing:

- **Water Bottle**: A **reusable water bottle** is not only eco-friendly but also practical for staying hydrated while exploring the city.
- **Snacks**: Pack a few **granola bars**, **nuts**, or a small pack of **trail mix** for when you're out and about.
- **Travel Pillow**: If you have a long journey to Bristol, a **travel pillow** can make your journey more comfortable.
- **Umbrella**: Bristol is known for its sporadic showers, so having a small **travel umbrella** tucked in your bag can help you avoid getting soaked.

6. Day Trip Essentials: Packing for Exploration

Bristol offers plenty of things to see and do, and you may want to take a day trip out to places like **Bath** or **Cheddar Gorge**. For these excursions, pack:

- **Day Backpack**: A small, lightweight backpack is perfect for carrying your snacks, water bottle, camera, and any extra layers for the day.
- **Guidebook or Map**: If you like exploring with a map, consider packing a **guidebook** or downloading an offline map on your phone for easy navigation.
- **Sunscreen and Bug Repellent**: If you're venturing outdoors for hiking or nature walks, pack **sunscreen** to protect

yourself from the sun and **bug repellent** if you're heading to areas with a lot of greenery.

Pro Tips for Packing Efficiently for 5 to 7 Days

- **Pack in Layers**: Bristol's weather can change rapidly, so make sure to pack clothes that can easily be layered for comfort.
- **Use Packing Cubes**: Organizing your clothes into packing cubes helps save space and keeps your suitcase organized.
- **Leave Room for Souvenirs**: If you plan on picking up souvenirs, try leaving a little extra space in your luggage.
- **Check the Weather Forecast**: Always check the weather forecast before packing to ensure you're ready for any changes in climate.

By packing efficiently, you'll be able to enjoy your 5-day or 7-day Bristol trip without the burden of overpacking. With versatile clothing, essential toiletries, and just the right amount of tech and documents, you'll be prepared to fully experience the city's charm, from its famous landmarks to hidden gems. Keep it simple, and your time in Bristol will be stress-free and unforgettable!

Seasonal Clothing Tips for Your Bristol Trip

Bristol is a city with a dynamic climate that changes with the seasons, so packing the right clothing for the time of year you're visiting is essential for comfort and enjoyment. Whether you're visiting in the brisk winter, pleasant spring, warm summer, or autumn, each season offers its own unique experiences and weather conditions. Here's a guide to packing clothing based on the season to help you make the most of your trip to Bristol.

Winter (December to February): Layer Up for Comfort

Winter in Bristol can be chilly, especially with the damp weather often common during these months. The temperature typically ranges from 3°C to 9°C (37°F to 48°F), but with wind and rain, it can feel colder. Therefore, layering is key to staying warm.

- **Warm Coat**: A **warm, waterproof winter coat** is essential to shield you from the elements. Opt for something insulated but not too bulky for easy movement.
- **Sweaters and Layering Pieces**: A couple of **cozy sweaters** or thermal tops will help you stay warm under your coat. Consider a **fleece-lined jacket** or a **cardigan** for extra warmth when indoors.
- **Thermal Leggings or Tights**: If you plan on wearing skirts or dresses, pair them with **thermal leggings** or tights to stay comfortable and warm.
- **Sturdy Waterproof Boots**: Bristol's streets can get slippery and wet during winter months, so pack **waterproof boots** with good traction to ensure comfort and safety when walking around.
- **Accessories**: Don't forget **a warm scarf**, **gloves**, and a **hat**. Woolen accessories will help keep you warm and stylish. A beanie or wool hat is perfect for protecting your head against the chill.

Spring (March to May): Light Layers and Rain Gear

Spring in Bristol is a beautiful time to visit, with temperatures ranging from 7°C to 15°C (45°F to 59°F). However, it's also a season of unpredictable weather—sunshine can quickly turn into rain showers. You'll want to pack a mix of light layers and rain gear to stay comfortable throughout the day.

- **Light Jacket or Waterproof Coat**: Pack a **lightweight waterproof jacket** or a **raincoat**. It will keep you dry during the frequent spring showers while still being breathable for warmer days.
- **Layered Tops**: Bring a few **long-sleeve shirts**, **t-shirts**, and

blouses that you can easily layer for warmth. You may want to add a **sweater** or a **cardigan** for chilly mornings or evenings.
- **Comfortable Jeans or Trousers**: You'll likely be doing a lot of walking, so pack **comfortable jeans** or **trousers**. If you're expecting warmer days, **lightweight cotton pants** or **skirts** will keep you cool.
- **Waterproof Footwear**: A pair of **water-resistant boots** or comfortable sneakers will serve you well when walking around town. Opt for something that can handle a bit of rain without getting soggy.
- **Umbrella**: A **compact travel umbrella** is a must in spring, as Bristol is known for its intermittent rainfall.

Summer (June to August): Pack for Warmth and Sun

Summer in Bristol is mild and pleasant, with average temperatures ranging from 14°C to 21°C (57°F to 70°F). On warmer days, temperatures can even rise to around 25°C (77°F). While you're likely to encounter plenty of sunshine, don't forget that temperatures can still dip during the evening or when you're in shaded areas. Here's what to pack for a summer visit:

- **Lightweight Clothing**: Bring **shorts**, **skirts**, and **dresses** for warmer days, paired with **light t-shirts**, **tank tops**, or **short-sleeve shirts**. Fabrics like cotton and linen are breathable and ideal for summer temperatures.
- **Comfortable Walking Shoes**: Since you'll probably be walking around a lot, make sure to pack **comfortable sandals** or **sneakers**. If you plan on dining out or attending an event, consider **dressy flats** or **loafers**.
- **Hat and Sunglasses**: Protect your eyes and face from the sun with a **wide-brimmed hat** and **sunglasses**. A sunhat will also help protect your scalp from sunburn.
- **Light Jacket or Sweater**: Even in summer, evenings can get cool, so having a **light cardigan** or **sweater** is recommended for comfort as the temperatures drop.
- **Sunscreen**: Don't forget to pack **sunscreen** with SPF 30+ to

protect your skin from harmful UV rays while enjoying the outdoors.

Autumn (September to November): Cozy Layers and Stylish Comfort

Autumn in Bristol can feel a bit crisp with temperatures ranging from 10°C to 18°C (50°F to 64°F), but it's still quite pleasant for sightseeing. The city's parks and streets become even more picturesque with the changing foliage, so this is a great time to explore.

- **Layered Clothing**: As the weather cools down, pack **long-sleeve shirts**, **sweaters**, and **light jackets** for easy layering. Consider a **fleece-lined jacket** or **puffer vest** for warmth.
- **Warm Pants or Jeans**: Bring **comfortable jeans**, **corduroy pants**, or **wool trousers**. These will keep you warm while maintaining a stylish autumn look.
- **Comfortable Boots**: Opt for **ankle boots** or **Chelsea boots** that will keep your feet warm while offering good support for long walks.
- **Scarf and Gloves**: A cozy **scarf** is a great accessory for layering in autumn, while **gloves** will help keep you warm on chillier days.
- **Rain Gear**: Since autumn can also be rainy in Bristol, be sure to pack a **water-resistant coat** or **umbrella** for any unexpected showers.

General Packing Tips for All Seasons

- **Pack Versatile Items**: Regardless of the season, try to choose clothing items that can be easily mixed and matched to create multiple outfits. Neutral colors work well, as they can be paired with just about anything.
- **Consider the Activities**: Think about the activities you'll be doing. If you plan on spending time outdoors, make sure to pack **comfortable walking shoes** and **weather-appropriate**

layers.
- **Leave Room for Souvenirs**: Bristol is home to a variety of quirky shops, so leave some extra space in your luggage for souvenirs or items you pick up during your trip.

By packing the right clothing for the season, you'll be ready to experience all that Bristol has to offer comfortably and stylishly. Whether you're braving the chill of winter or soaking up the sun during summer, you'll be prepared for any weather the city throws your way!

About the Author

Samuel F. Justin is a travel enthusiast and accomplished author of comprehensive travel guides. With years of exploring diverse cultures and destinations, he shares insightful expertise on cultural immersion, historical landmarks, culinary delights, and outdoor adventures. His passion for storytelling inspires travelers to discover new horizons.

Printed in Great Britain
by Amazon